Introduction

All the mazes in this book share a common theme: the alphabet. There are two reasons that I chose this connecting theme. First, I enjoy letters so much that I have spent thousands of hours as a typographer, a designer of letters. Typography has been more than a hobby but far less than a career or profession. Second, this collection of mazes was fairly easy to do because I had developed many of its specialized maze typefaces for another book, **Easy Alphabet Mazes,** designed for small children. The potential of the specialized typefaces used in that book could not be realized in very easy mazes, so this follow-up seemed appropriate.

The goal of this book is to provide entertainment for people who enjoy mazes. There is no claim of educational value; any person who can do these mazes has long ago mastered the alphabet. If you are looking for books to help young children learn their letters with the aid of mazes, do consider **Easy Alphabet Mazes.**

This book has four parts. The first 26 mazes have the shape of a letter of the alphabet and are made up of elements of that letter. They are all fairly easy mazes. The second part, called More Alphabet Mazes, has 35 mazes using other ways to construct mazes from the letters of the alphabet. Most of the mazes in this part use tessellation patterns. In the third part, called Bonus Alphabet Mazes, some patterns that had been used earlier in the book get a second chance. Most of these 19 mazes are more difficult than those earlier in the book. In addition, each of these mazes has a solve-it-twice feature: a second set of entry/exit points are given so each maze has two different solutions. The fourth and final section contains solutions to the mazes in the first three sections. Solutions are shown with all the dead-end passages blocked up, leaving only the correct path.

These mazes were produced using software programs that I developed two decades ago, partly to produce two books of mazes that Dover Publications published, **Fascinating Mazes** (1994) and **Maze Madness** (1996). The programs generate a maze as an array of numbers and then convert the numbers into a set of letters, which allows the maze to be displayed with the special maze typefaces that I construct.

I hope you enjoy solving these mazes as much as I have enjoyed designing them. I apologize in advance for any errors that remain in this book.

Robert Schenk
February 2012

PS If you enjoy these mazes, check out **Tantalizing Tessellating Mazes.**

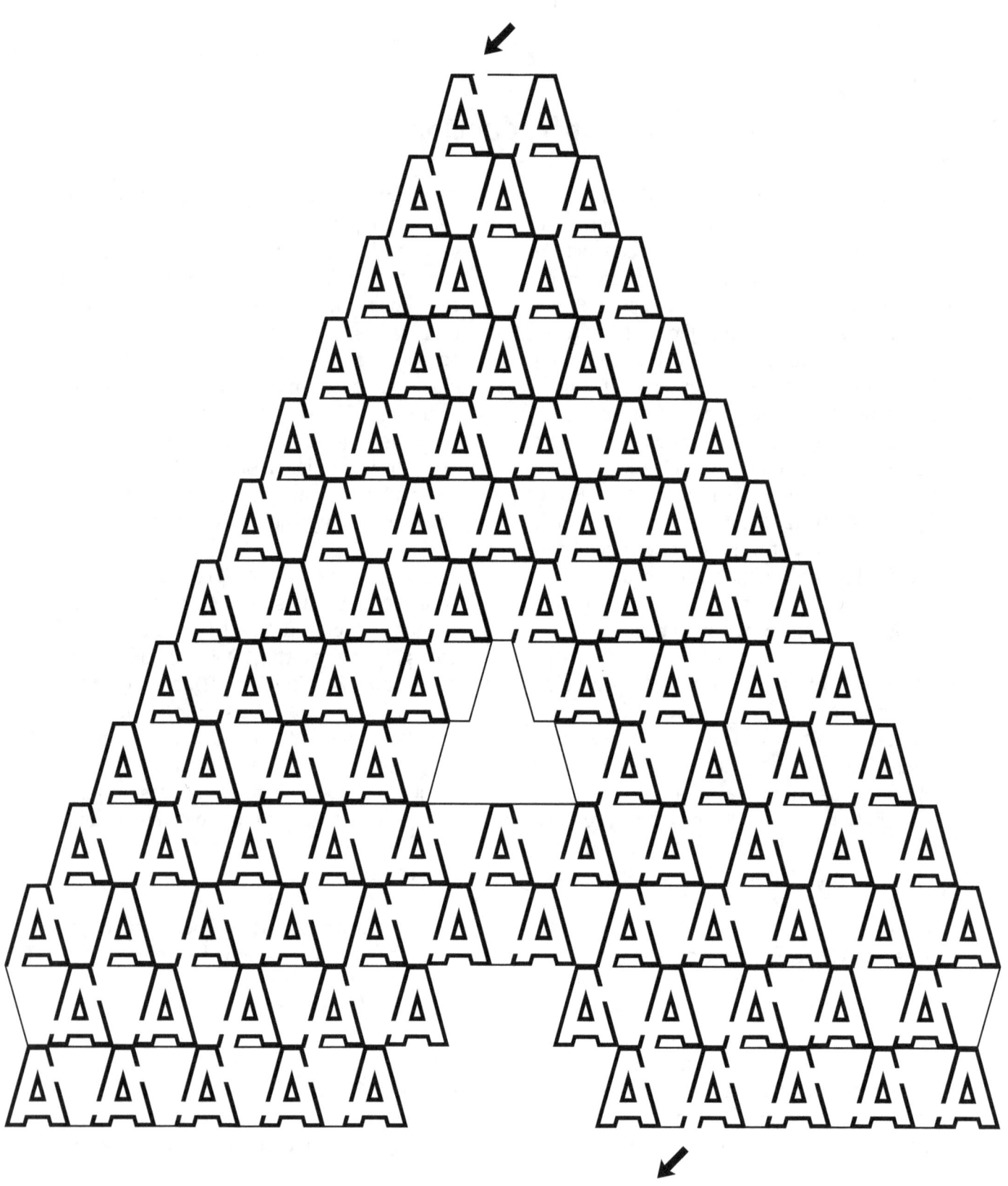

An A mAze to stArt An Amusing And AmAzing Adventure.

Stay Between the Borders from top to Bottom.

C

ConneCt from C to shining C.

6

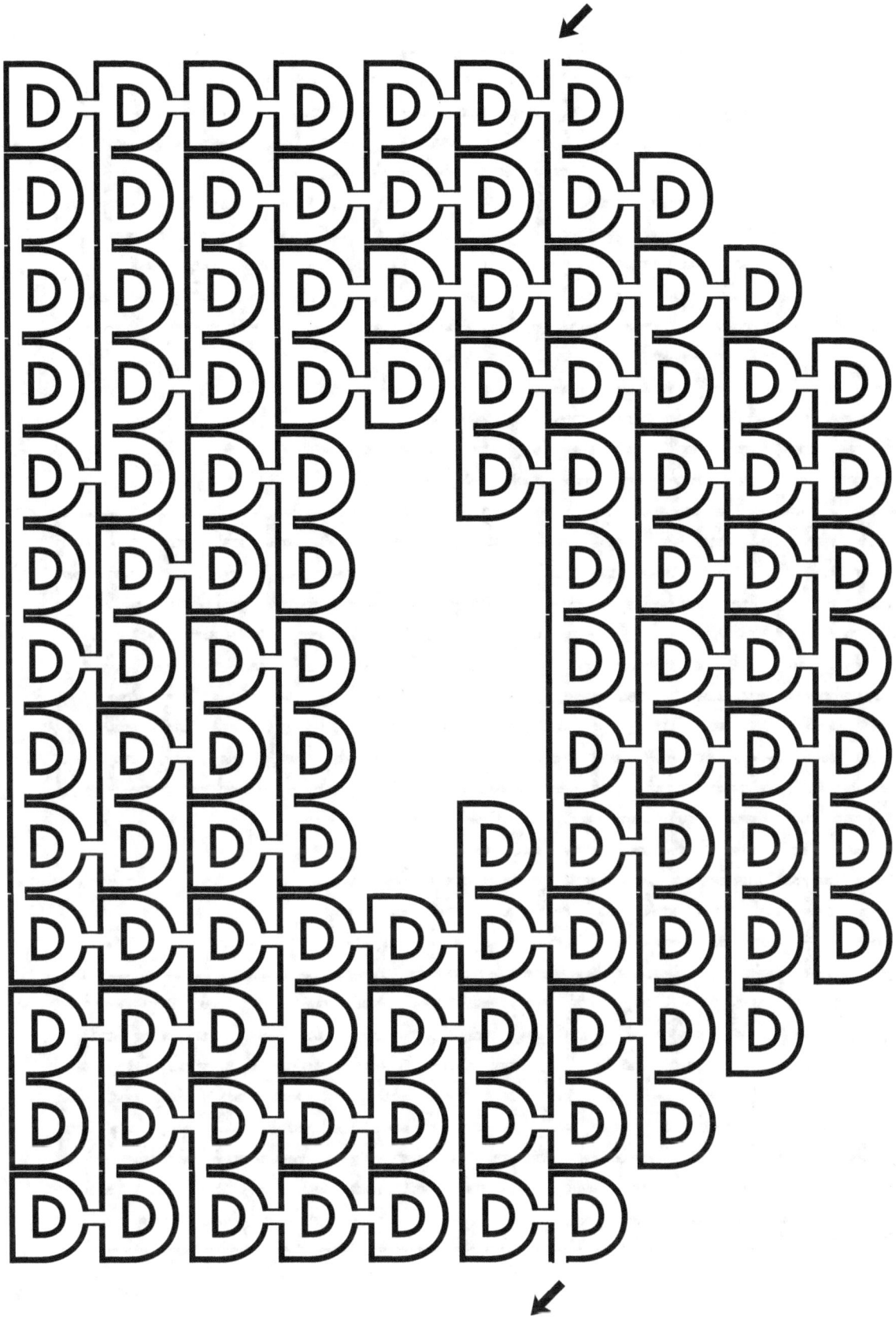

Determine the Desired Destination anD Don't Detour as you Drive to it.

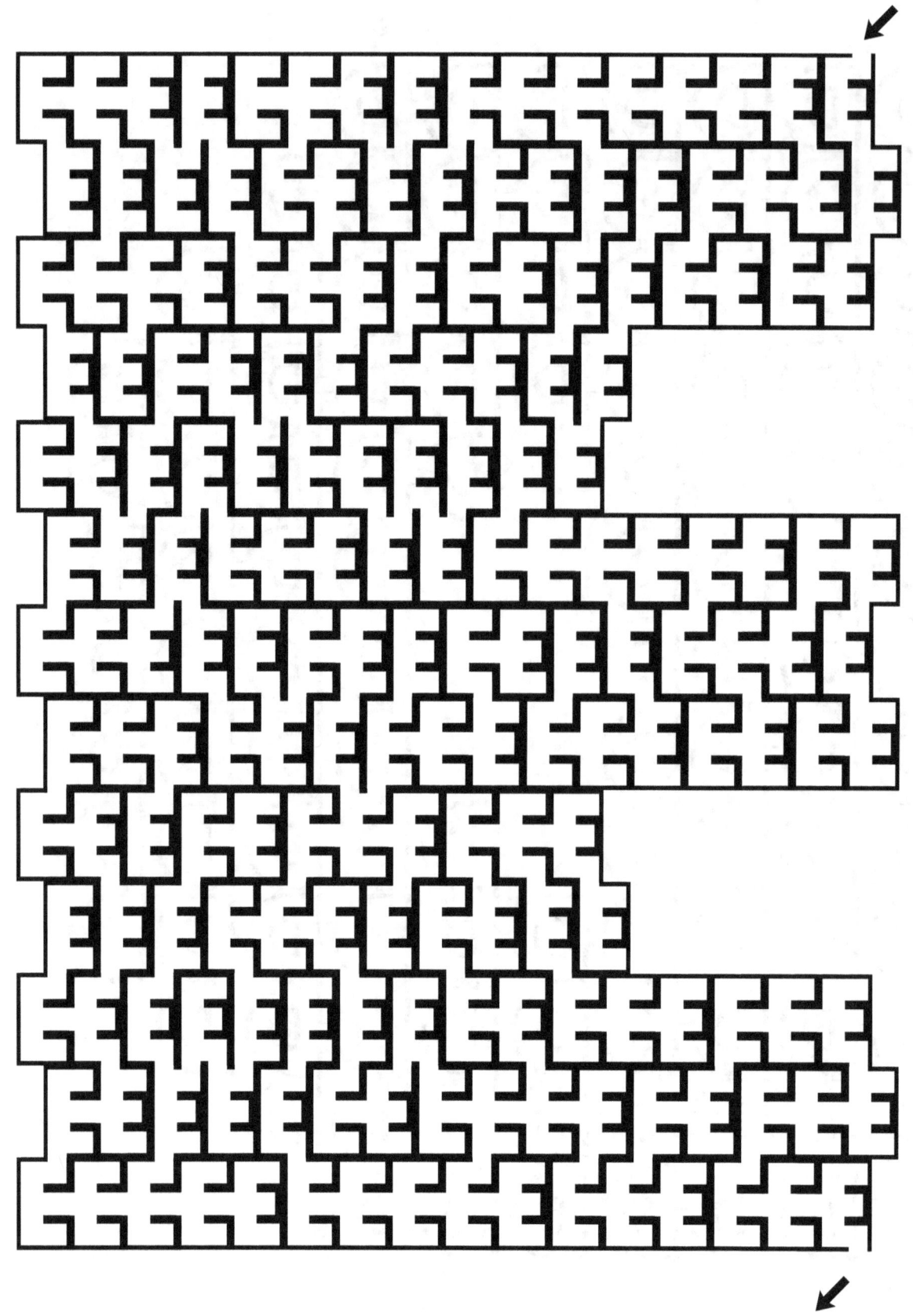

E could bE EasiEr.

How difFicult can Finding a path From top to bottom be?

Gloat after closinG the Gap in this Grid of Gs.

AHHH. THe Horizontal, HaugHty H. Start HigH, finisH low.

This Tessellating I Is Intriguing.

Your Job (obJective) is Just to Join top to bottom. EnJoy your Jog.

Check out these Kicking Ks.

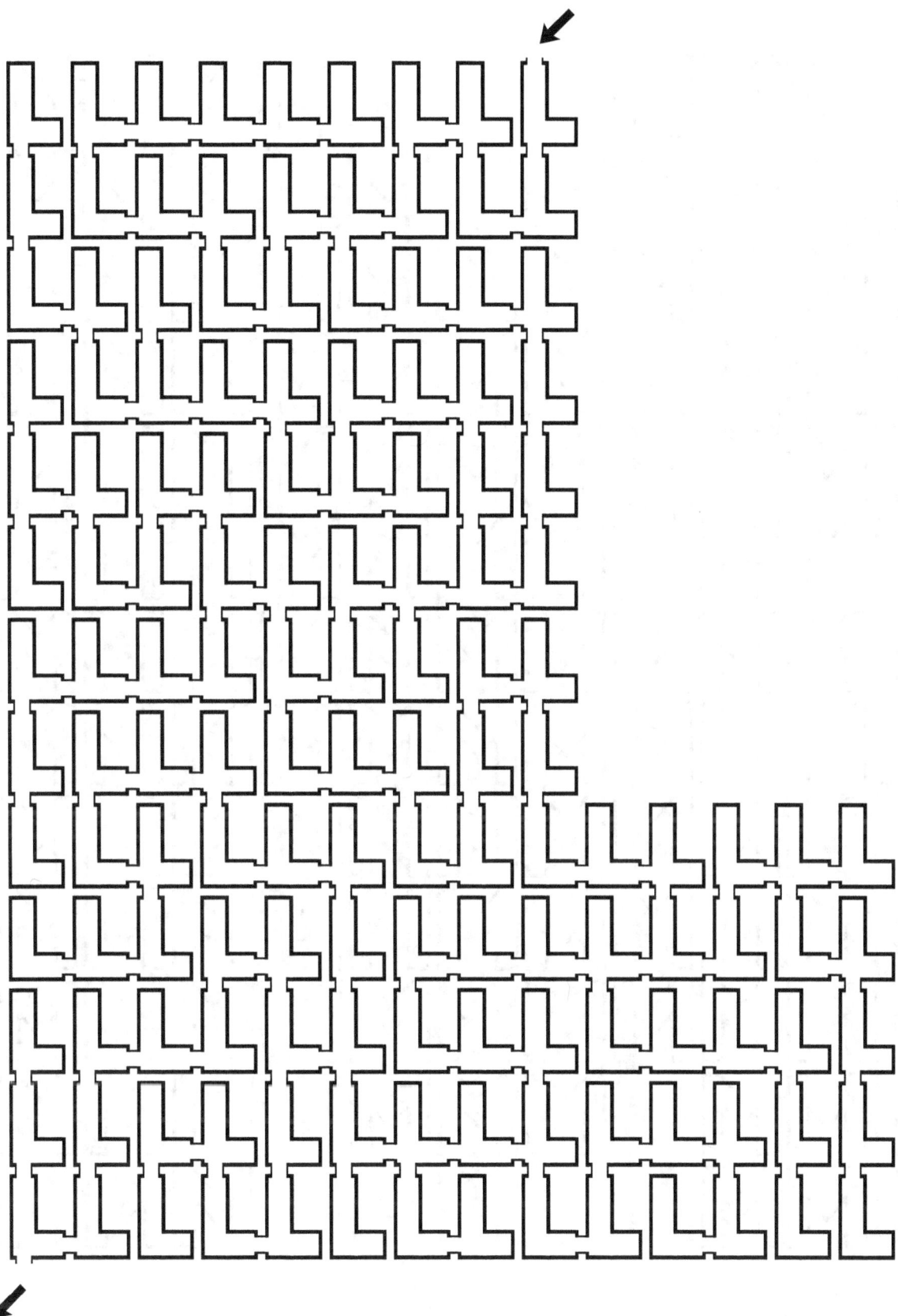

Locate the line that allows leaving the labyrinth.

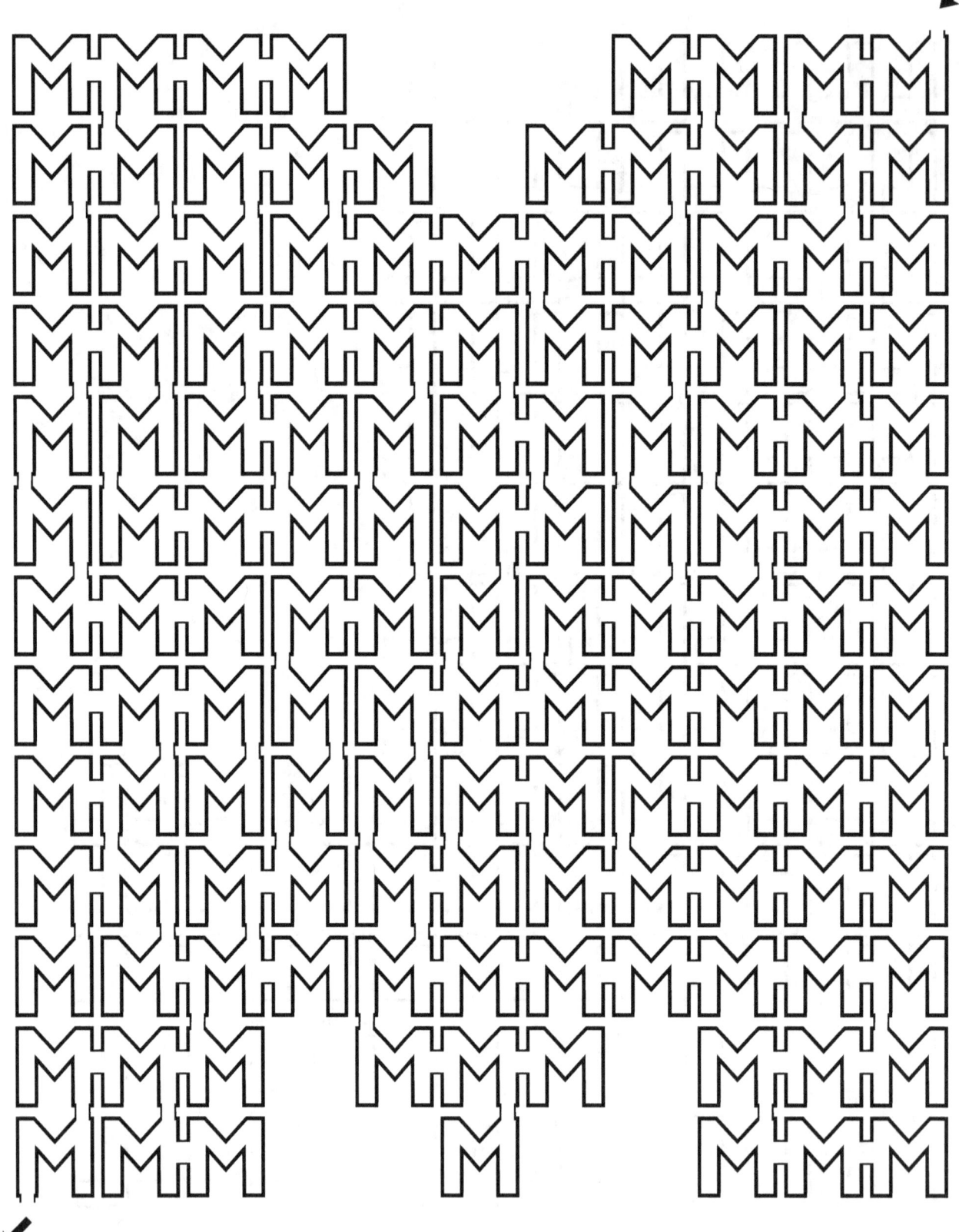

Master the Mangled M Maze in MiniMuM tiMe.

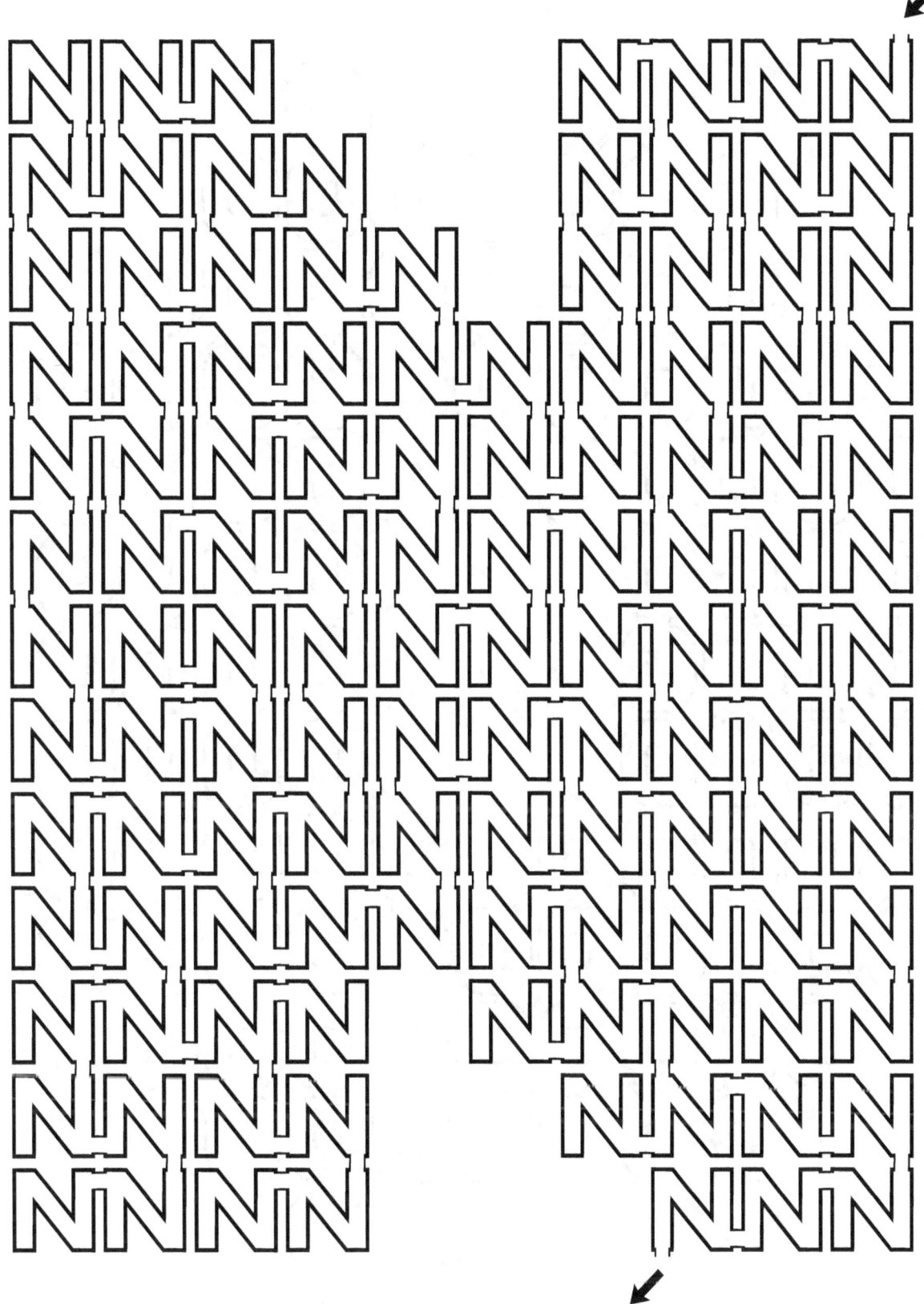

neatly pencil in a line to connect the arrows.

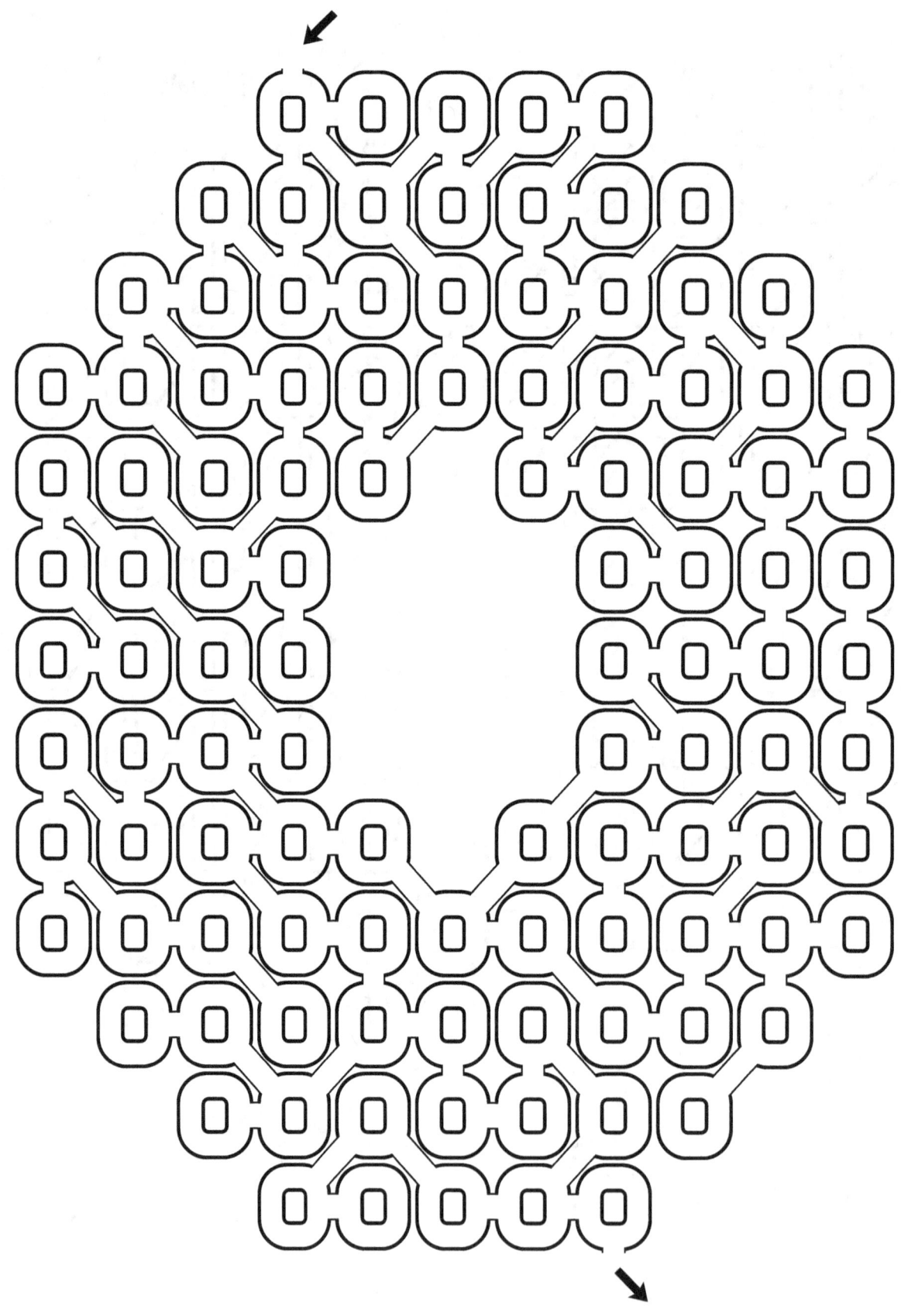

Follow along in hollow Os from top to bottom.

18

P

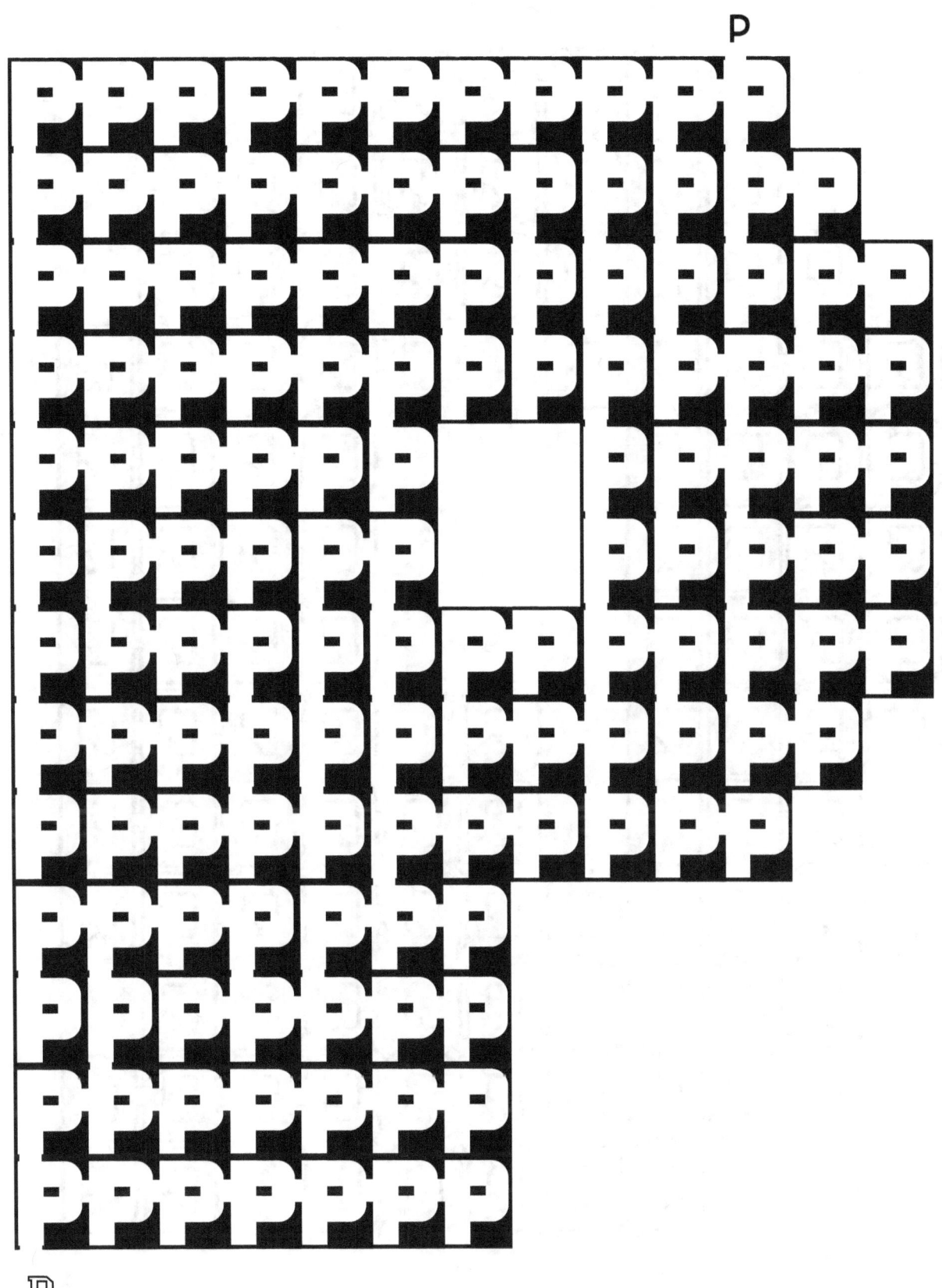

P

Pencil a Path from P to shining P in this Plain P Puzzle.

19

InQuiring minds Question if you can Quickly complete your Quest to solve the uniQue Q maze.

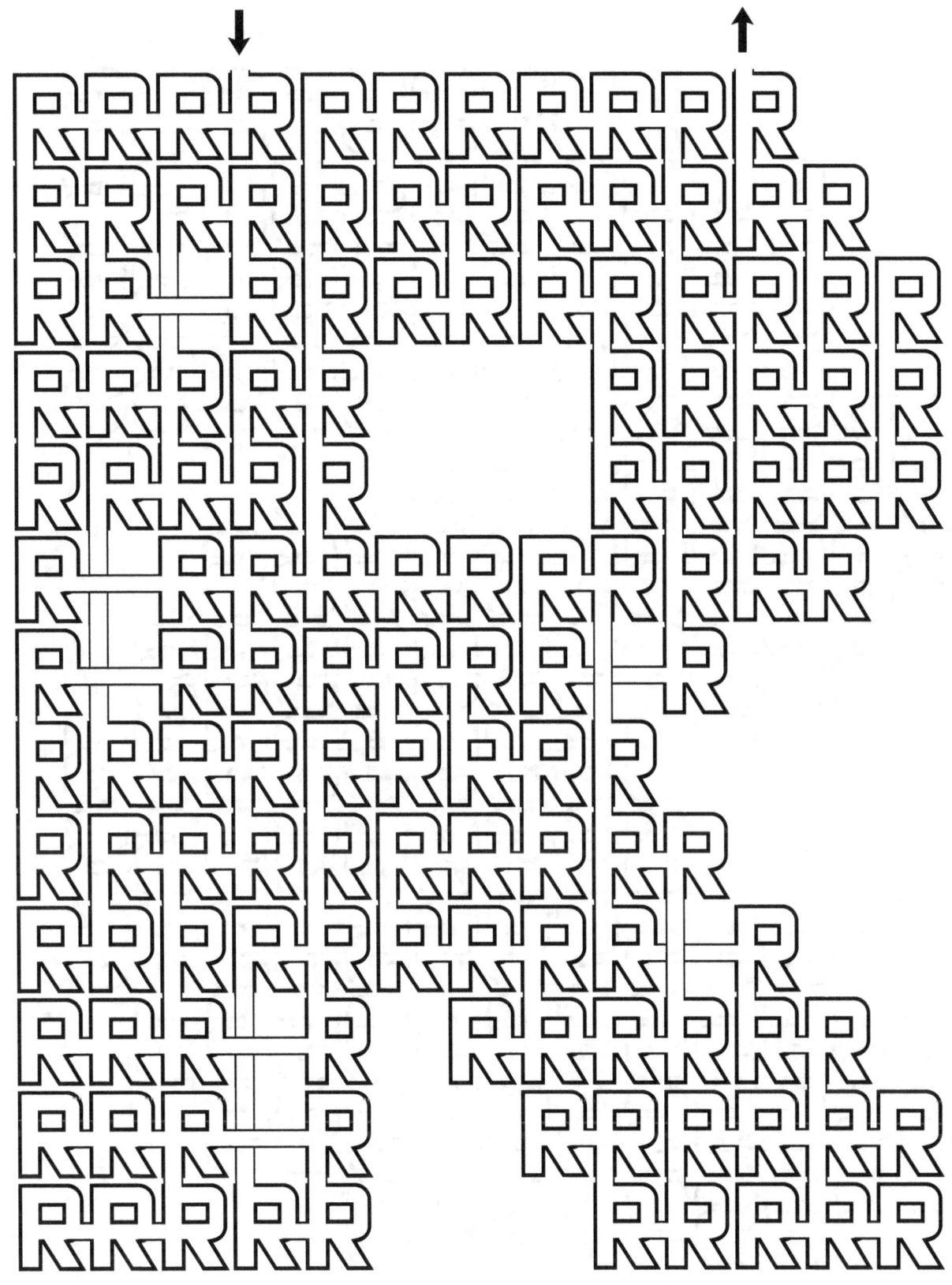

An oveR and undeR tRek. Don't Ramble, RepaiR eRRoRs, and aRRive back at the top.

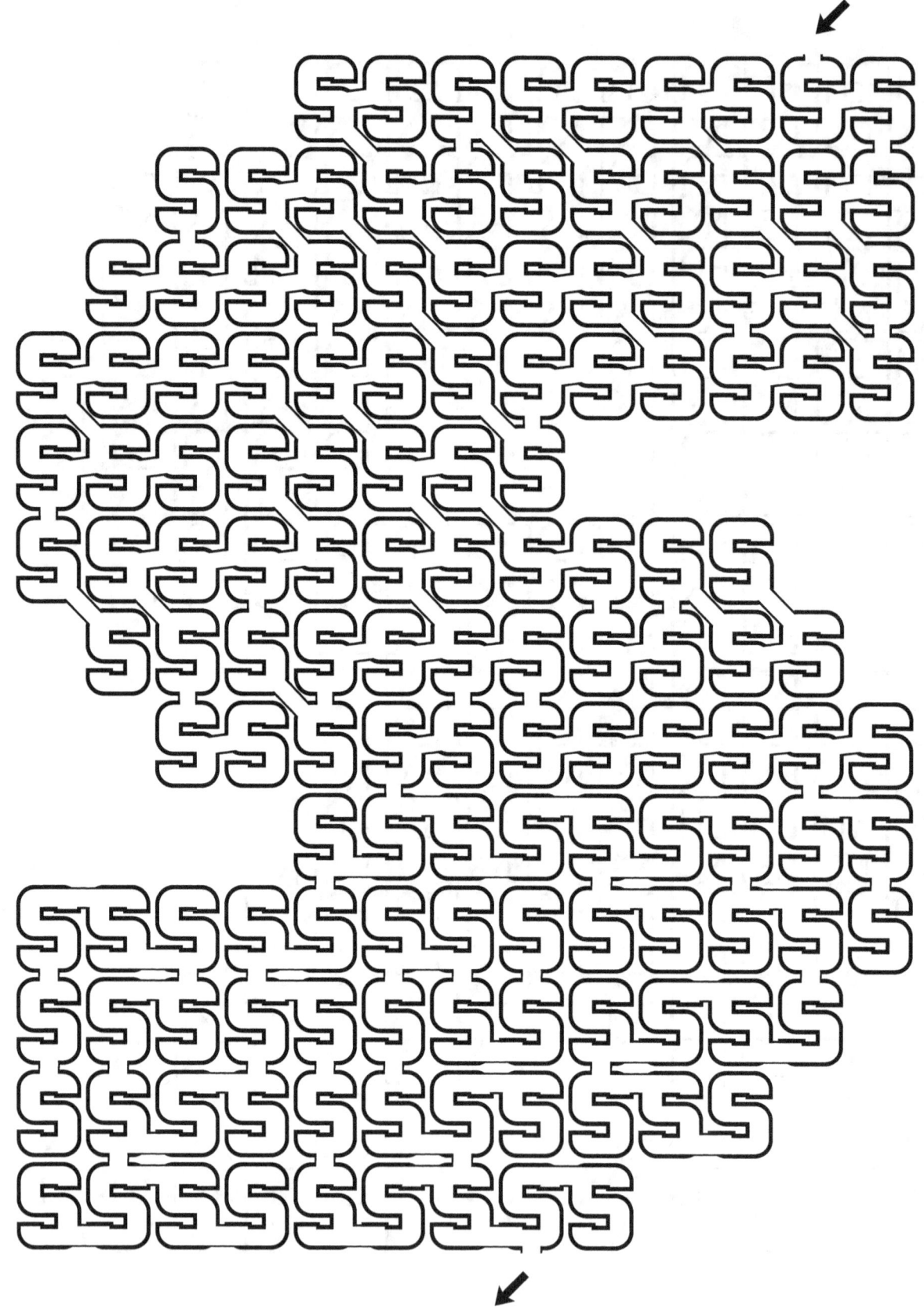

Sophisticated S has a top that differs from its bottom. See the Split?

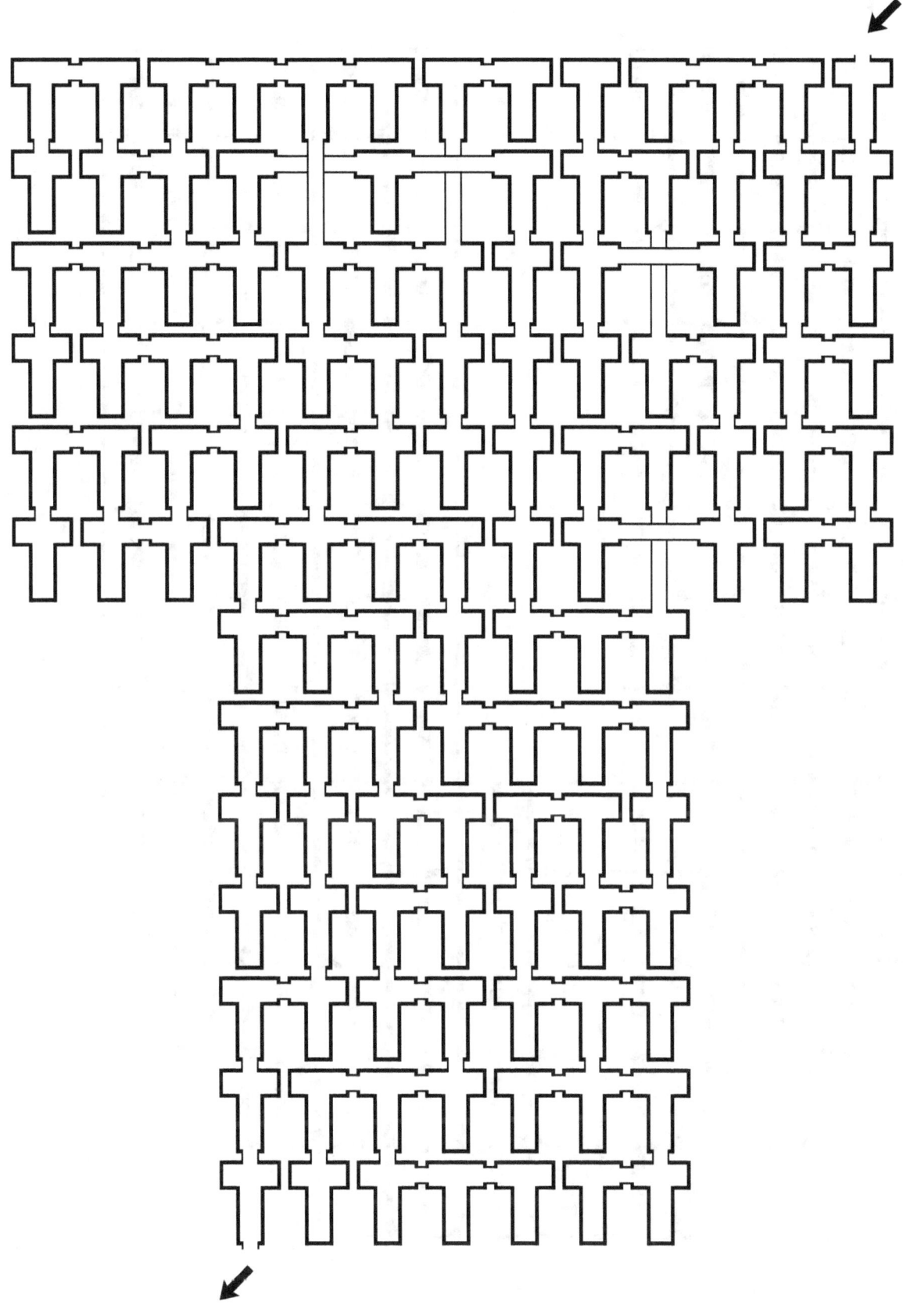

Full ThroTTle Through The sTraighT T.

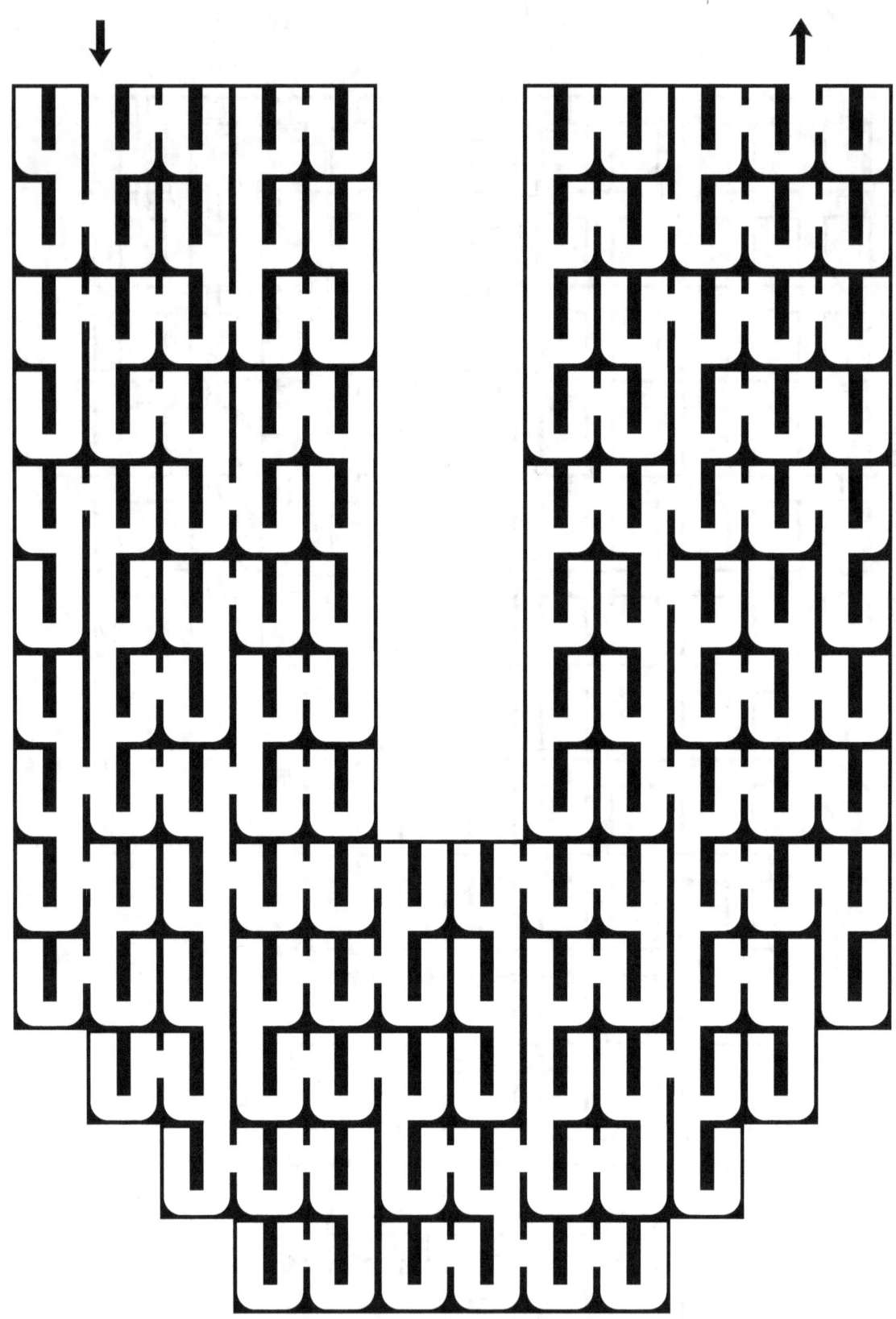

Unite stems with a UniqUe, Unbroken line.

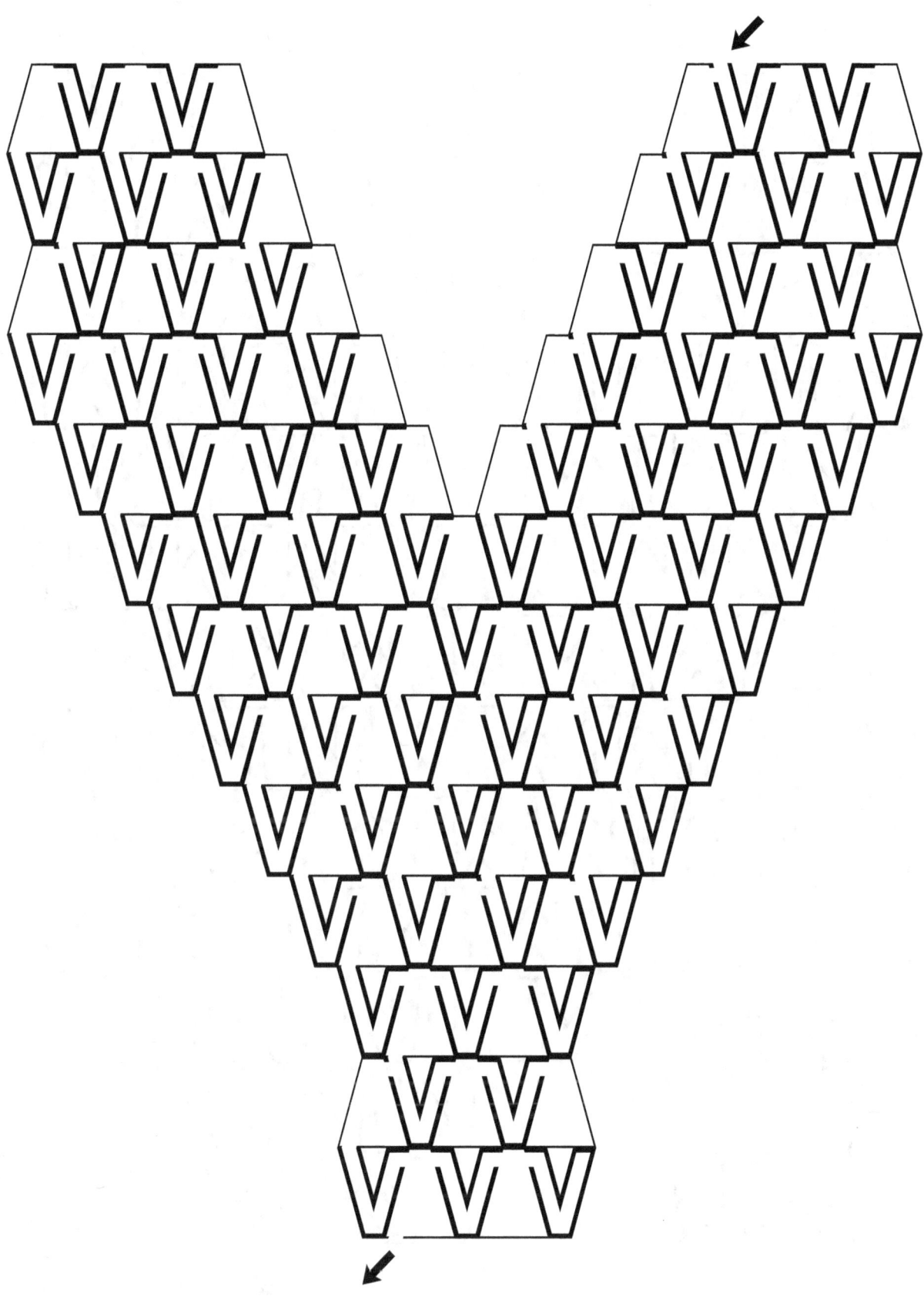

A Valley of Vs can be Very Vexing.

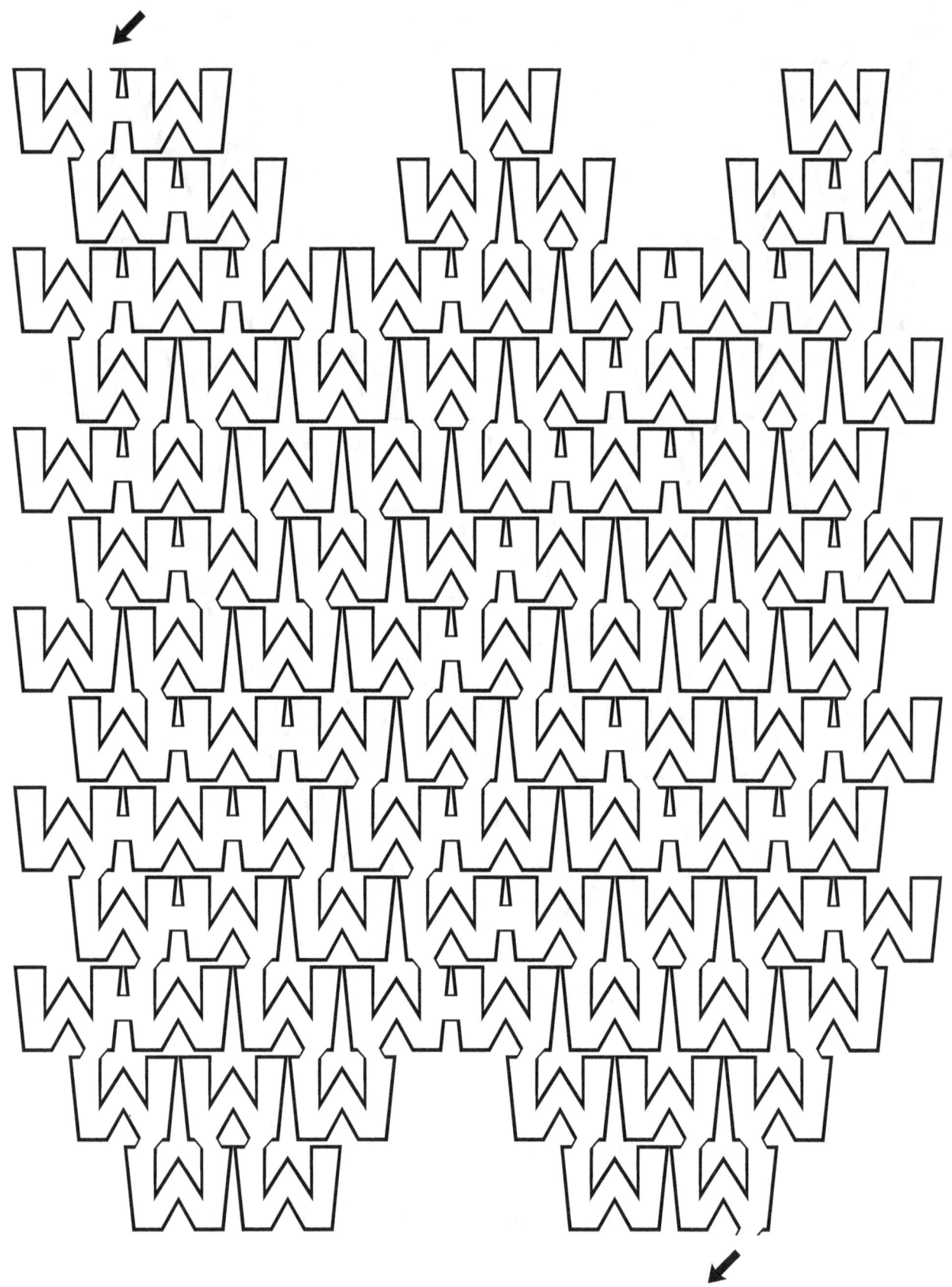

Wind your Way toWard the LoWer outlet Without Wandering off course.

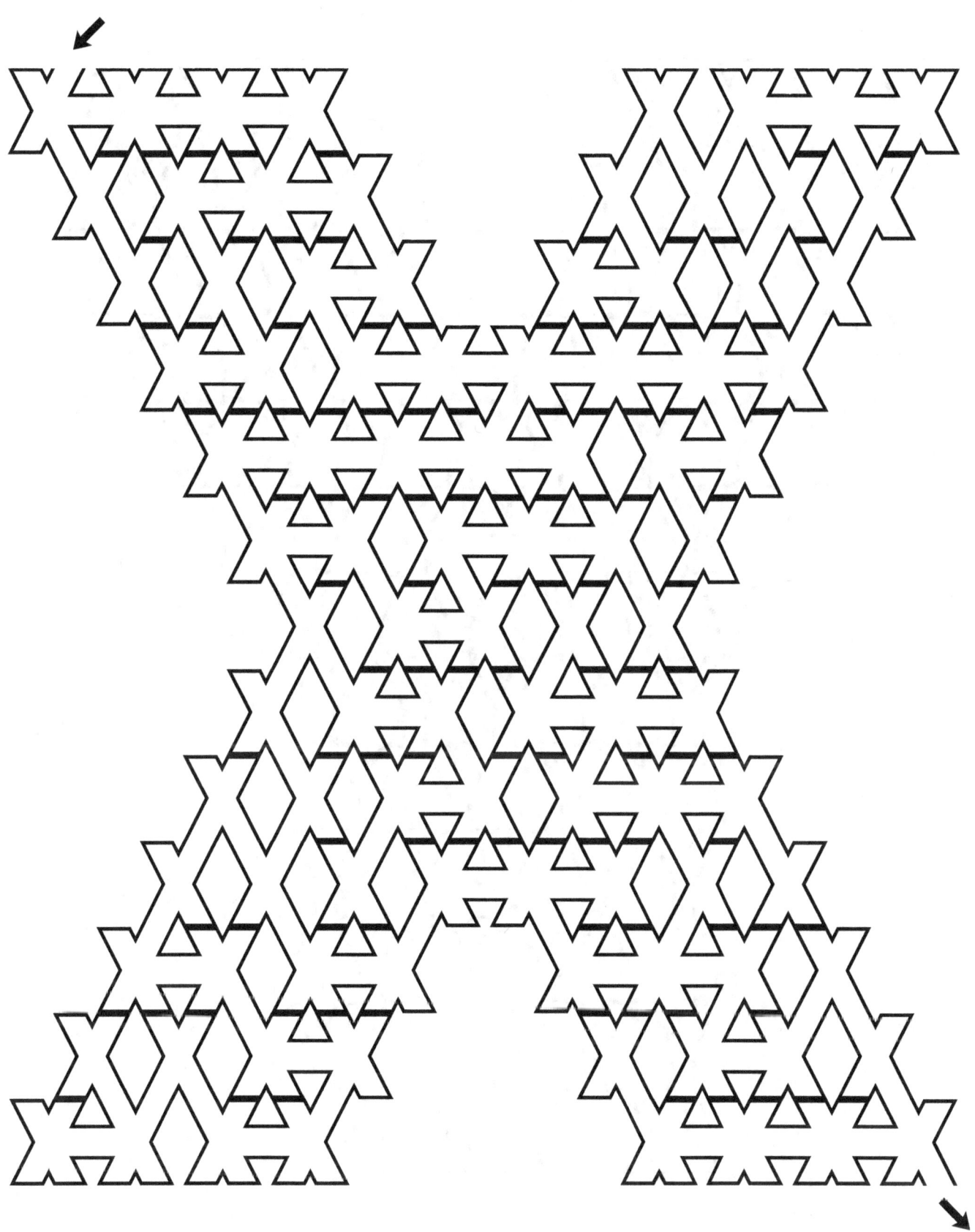

EXperience the heXagonal eXcellence of the X maze.

You won't feel YuckY if You hurry through this labYrinth.

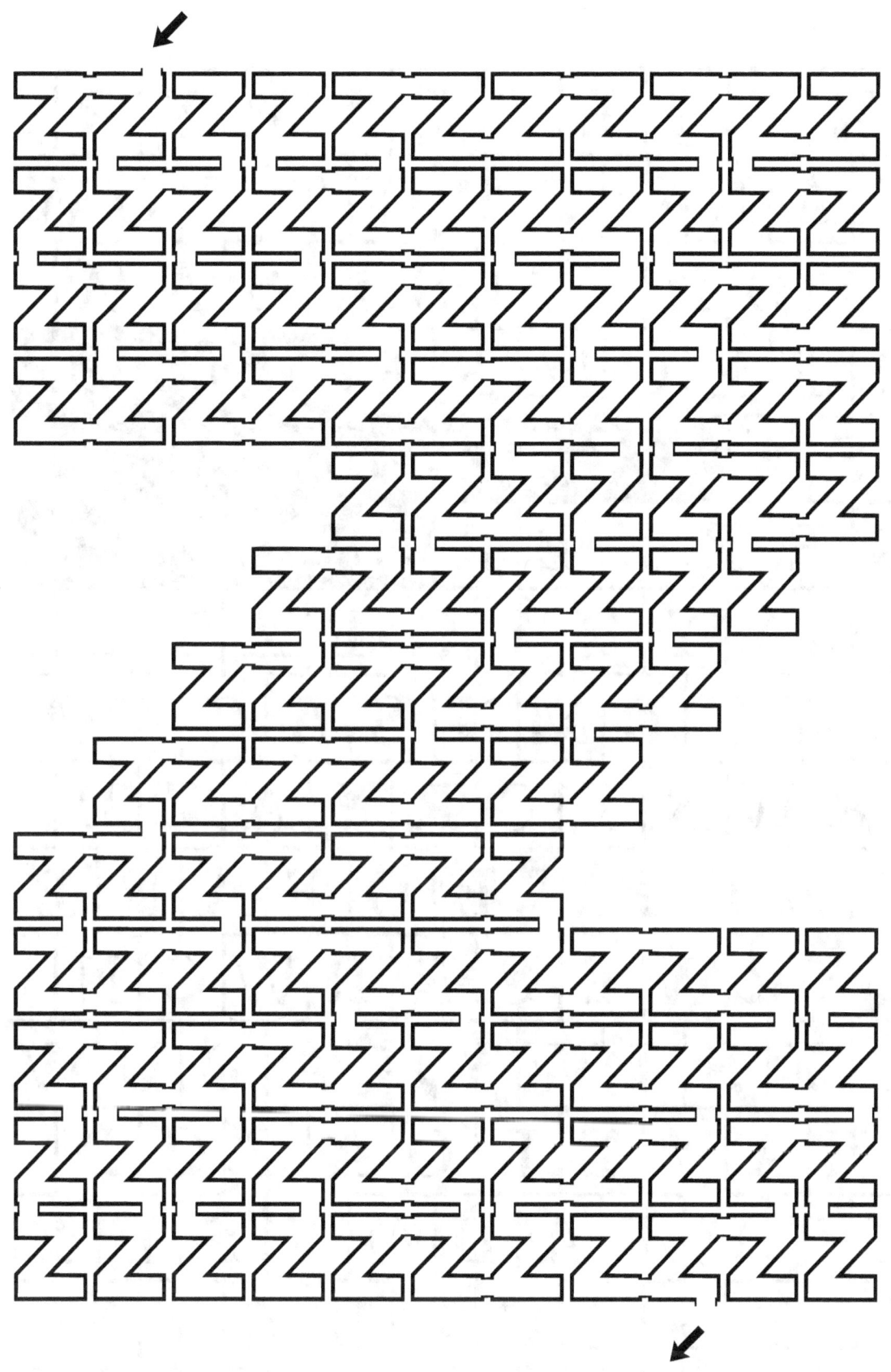

Are you buZZing with Zeal and Zest to conquer the Z maze?

MORE ALPHABET MAZES

This is as close to tessellating Bs as I could get.

Can you see the Cs in this maze?

32

More tessellating Cs.

33

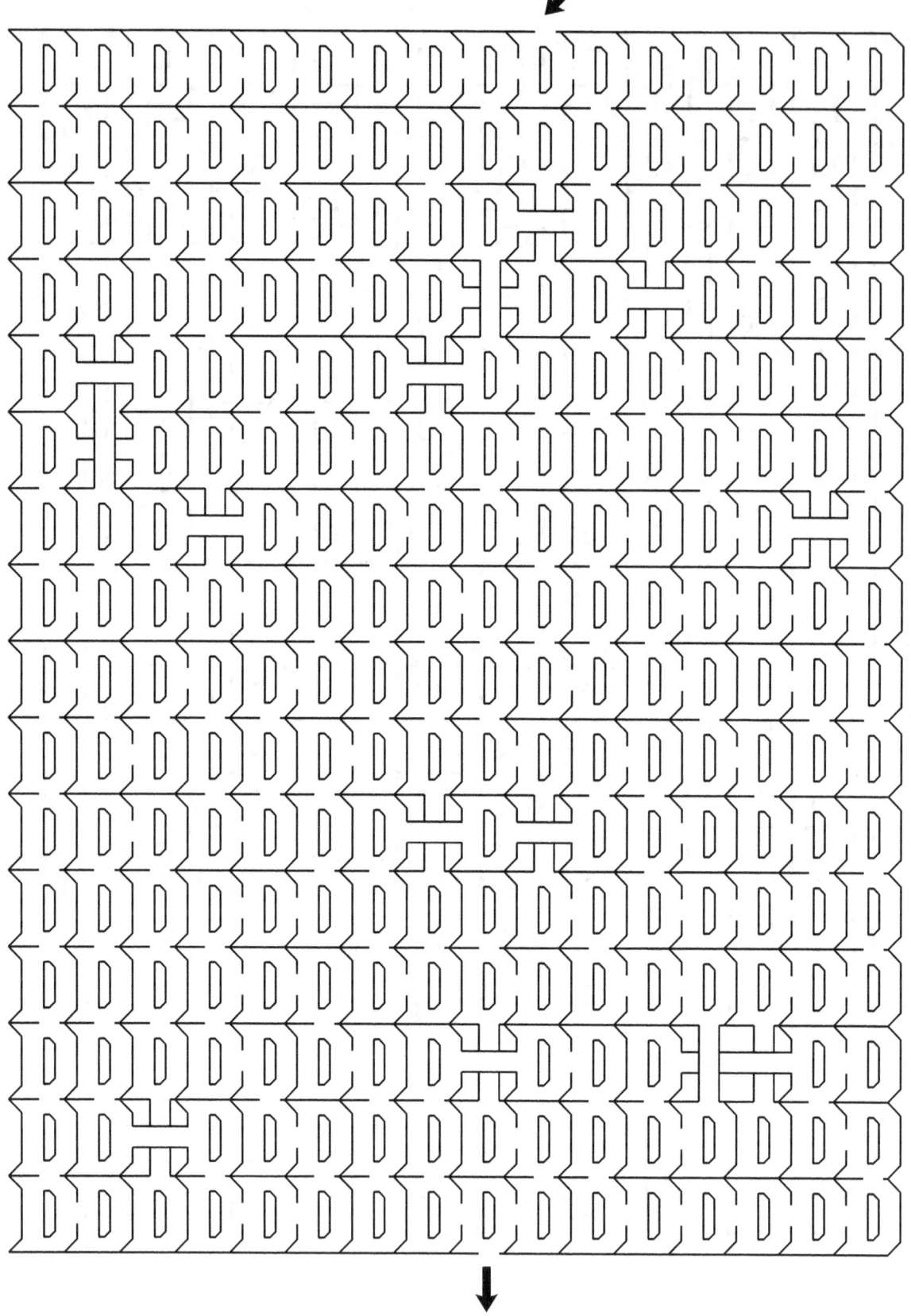

The letter D in a pseudo-tessellation pattern, with a few overpasses and underpasses.

34

Getting the Es to tessellate was not hard. Figuring out how to use them in a maze was.

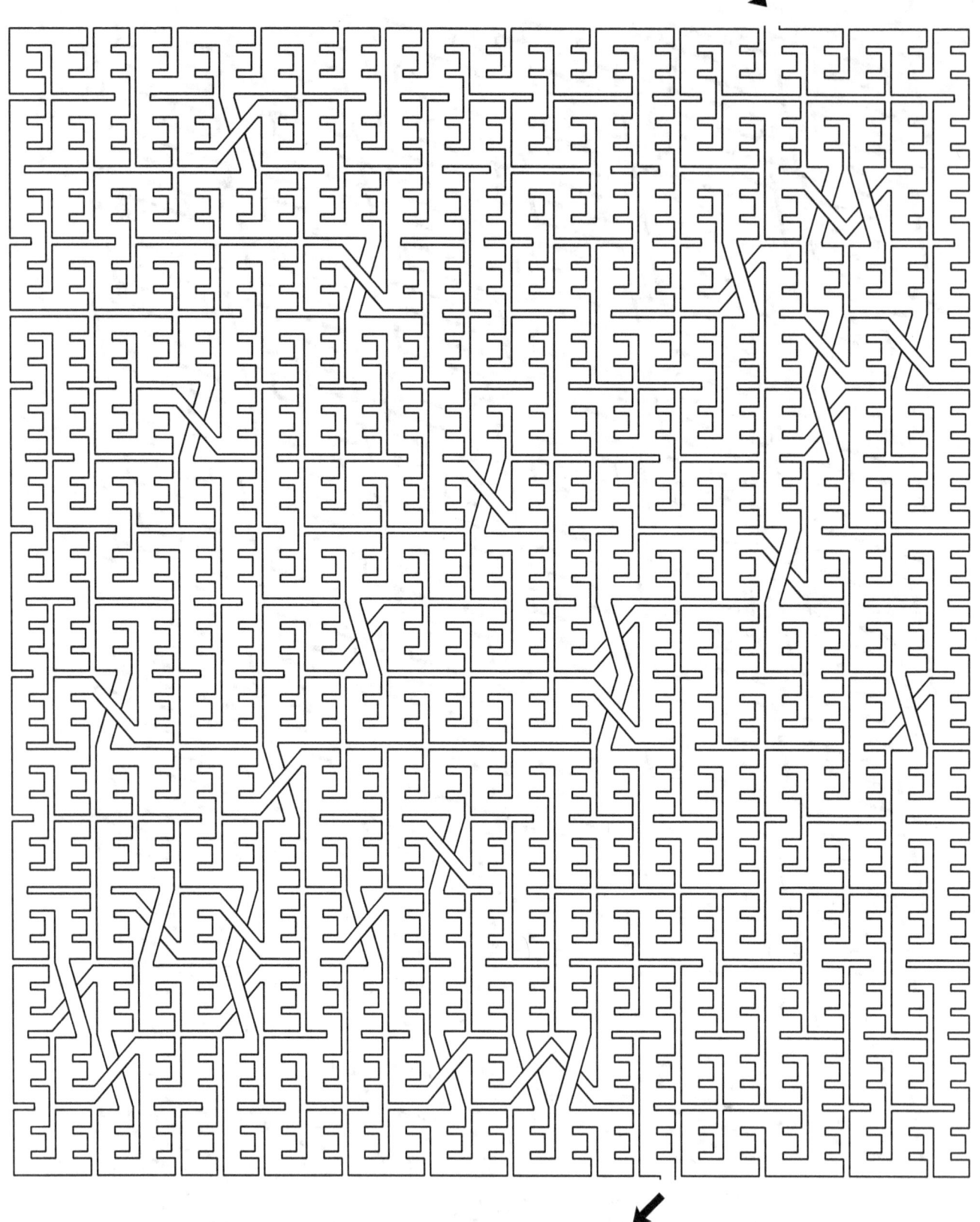

This maze with underpasses and overpasses looks more challenging than it actually is.

A tessellation is a form that fits together to fully fill an infinite flat surface. The F is flipped horizontally and vertically.

An oddly shaped F that tessellates.

Tessellating Gs make challenging mazes.

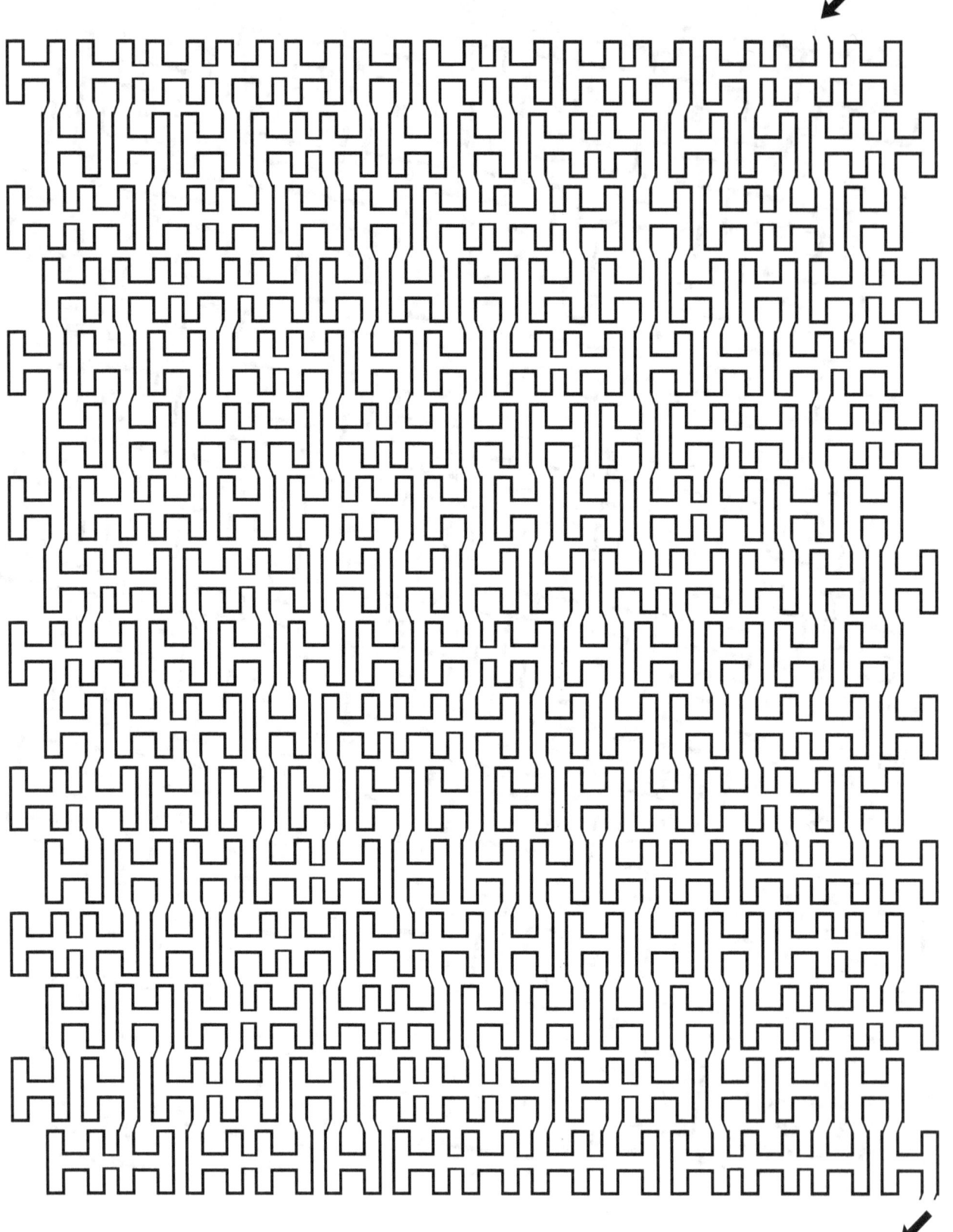

Hexagonal Hs--each H can connect to six neighbors.

Tessellating Hs can make even simple mazes hard.

This maze is based on a simple tessellation pattern of the letter I. Made into a maze, It can look Nazi, but denazification hides the tessellation pattern.

A Tuscan I, with a split serif, is another solution to the problem of tessellating the
I.

J tessellates and makes easy mazes difficult.

Don't let blocks of Ks keep you trapped.

L tessellates in several ways. Here is one.

An M maze in the middle of an amusing maze adventure.

I hope overcoming those interlocked Os provides oodles of enjoyment.

Interlocking Os form good mazes.

An attempt to tesselate Ps, it could also be a set of b, d, p, and q. Or 69. Or 96.

Pseudo-tessellating Qs.

The challenge in making this maze was not tessellating the Ss. It was getting them aligned so they would work in a maze.

One way to tessellate Ts.

A different way to tessellate Ts.

54

A third T-tessellation pattern. There are more.

Unusual U fun for you.

Tessellating Us can be confusing.

Tessellating Vs also make interesting mazes.

If you flipped it over, it could be a maze of tessellating Ms.

A decorative X pattern.

An extra X maze: Xs extending across the plane, fitting exactly--tessellations.

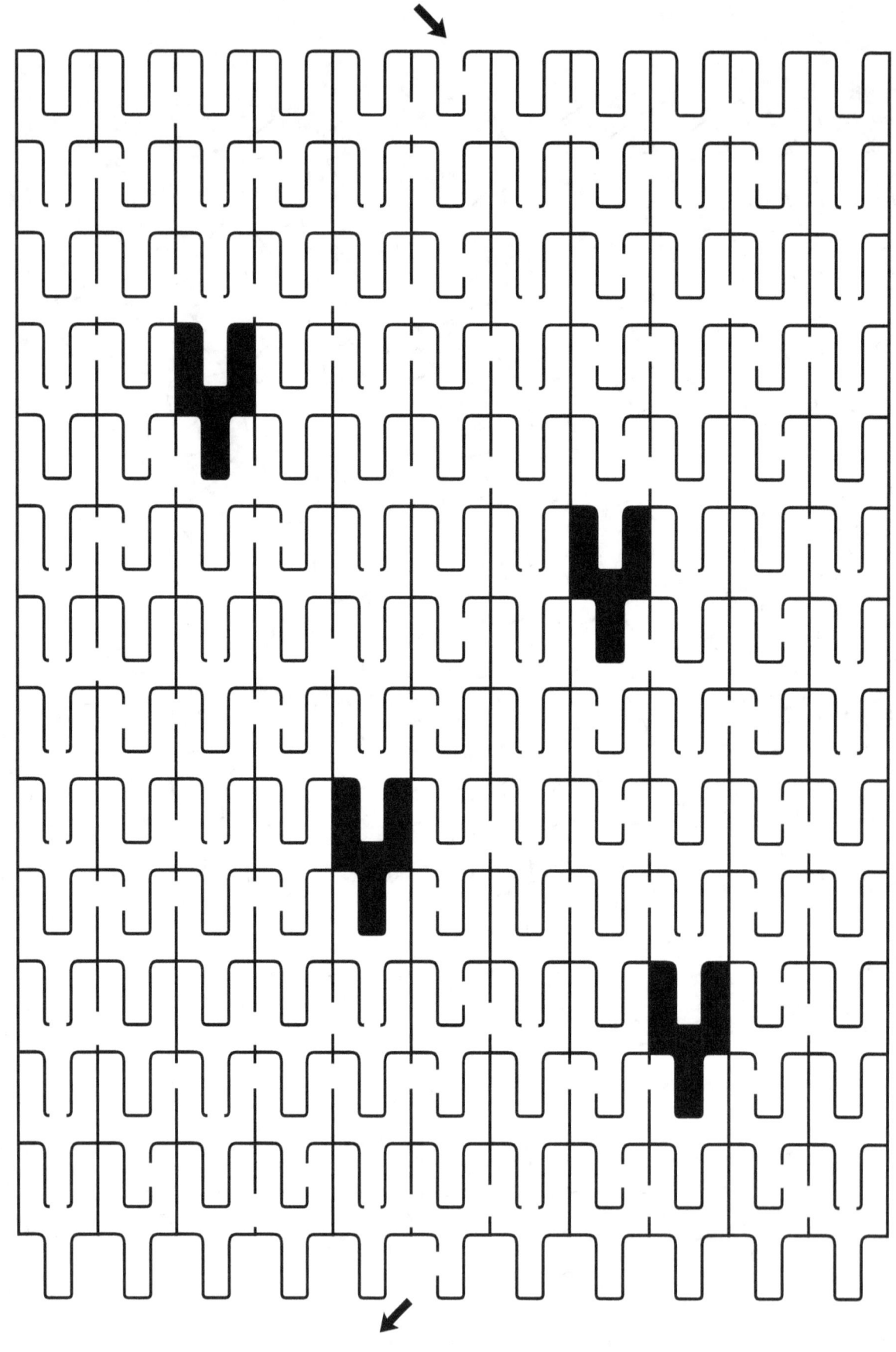

y will tessellate if it is squared off a bit.

A Z-maze, not an eZZie maze.

A bizarre puzzle of tessellating Zs ends our zigzagging adventure.

BONUS SECTION

I have almost run out of ideas for interesting alphabet maze fonts, but not out of pages. (Create Space, a division of Amazon that publishes this book, charges the same for a book that has 108 pages as for a book with 80. Or 60. Or 35.) This section is a chance to recycle (it is always good to recycle, isn't it?) some previously used alphabet maze fonts in mazes that are more challenging than those earlier in the book. The mazes also have a special feature: an alternate pair of exits, shown by the pointy fingers, allows you to solve the maze twice. (Solutions are shown at the end.)

The first of six fairly similar over-under mazes. It is also a work-'em-twice maze.

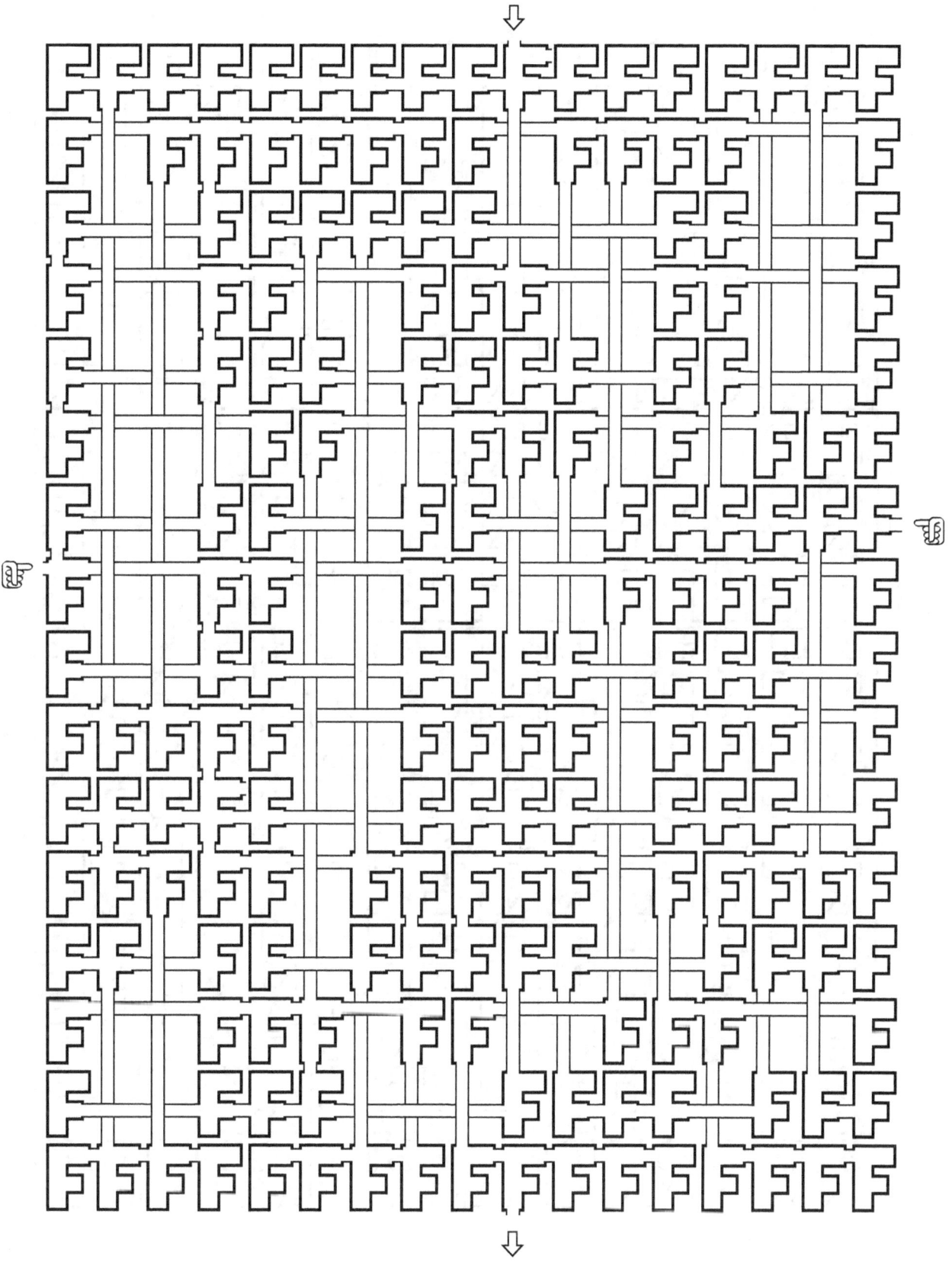

Fun starts with F.

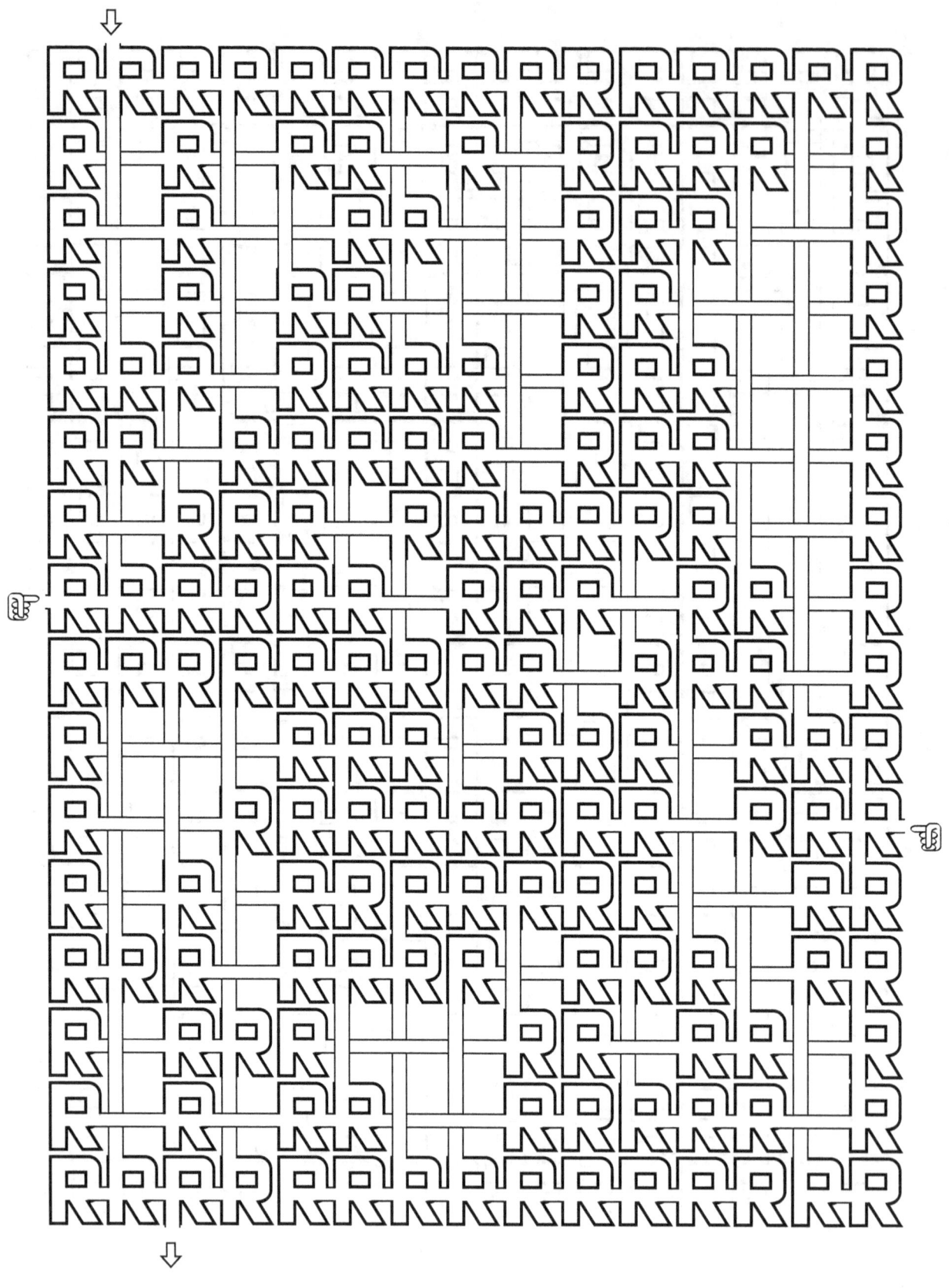

Remember, all the mazes in this bonus section can be solved twice.

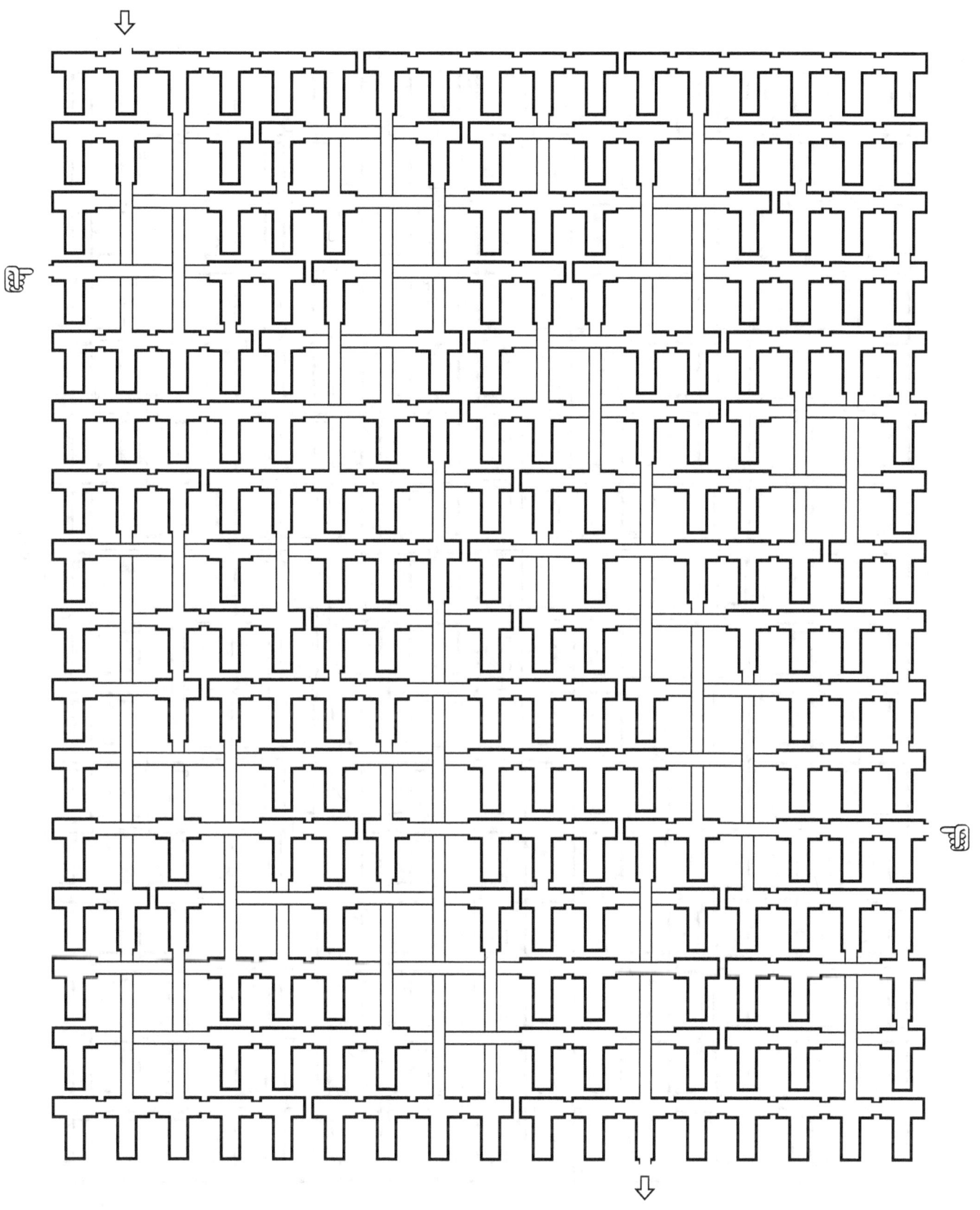

Trip, trek, and travel start with T.

The penultimate over/under maze of this series.

The last letter of the alphabet and the last of the over-under mazes (for a few pages).

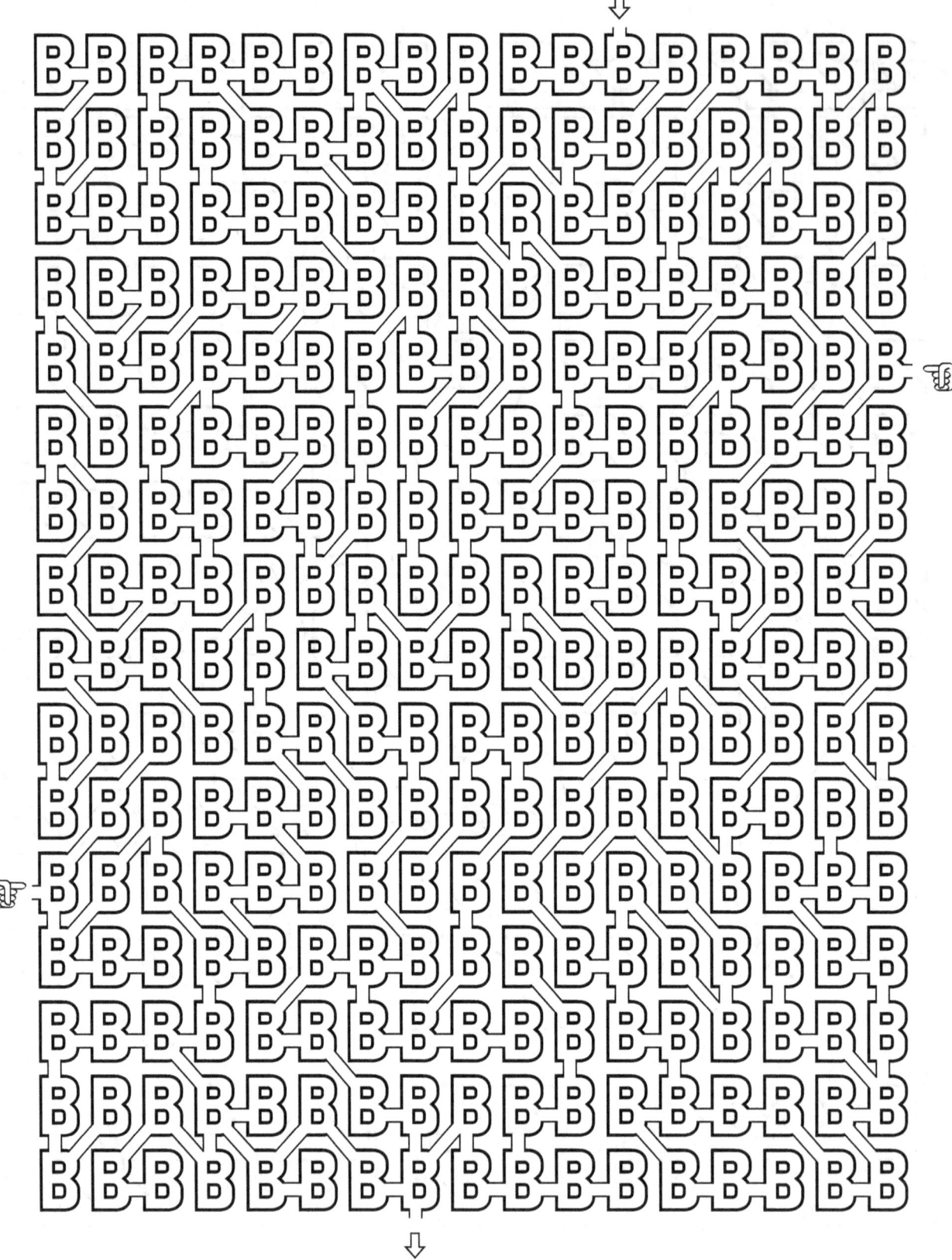

Now for some mazes that can connect diagonally as well as horizontally and vertically.

In these mazes each letter can connect to eight neighbors.

Remember, all the mazes in this bonus section can be solved twice.

Only one direction of diagonal can appear in this maze.

The last of the octo-mazes, mazes in which connections to eight neighbors are possible.

76

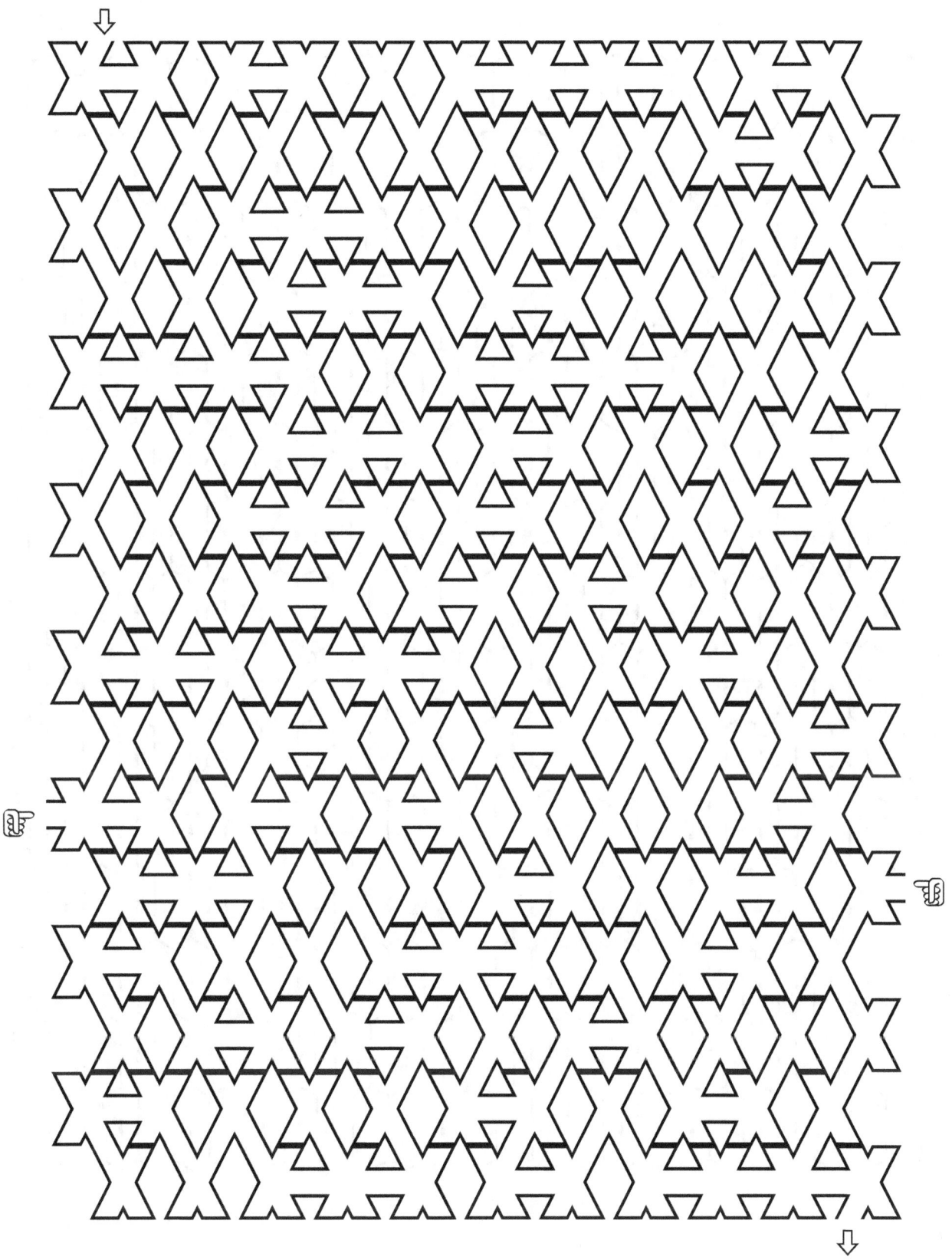

X has nice symmetry. It and the next two mazes can connect to any six neighbors.

This was the best I could do for tessellating Os. However, the pattern does make a good maze.

This has the same shape as an earlier maze, but the connections are different. It can connect to any of six neighbors.

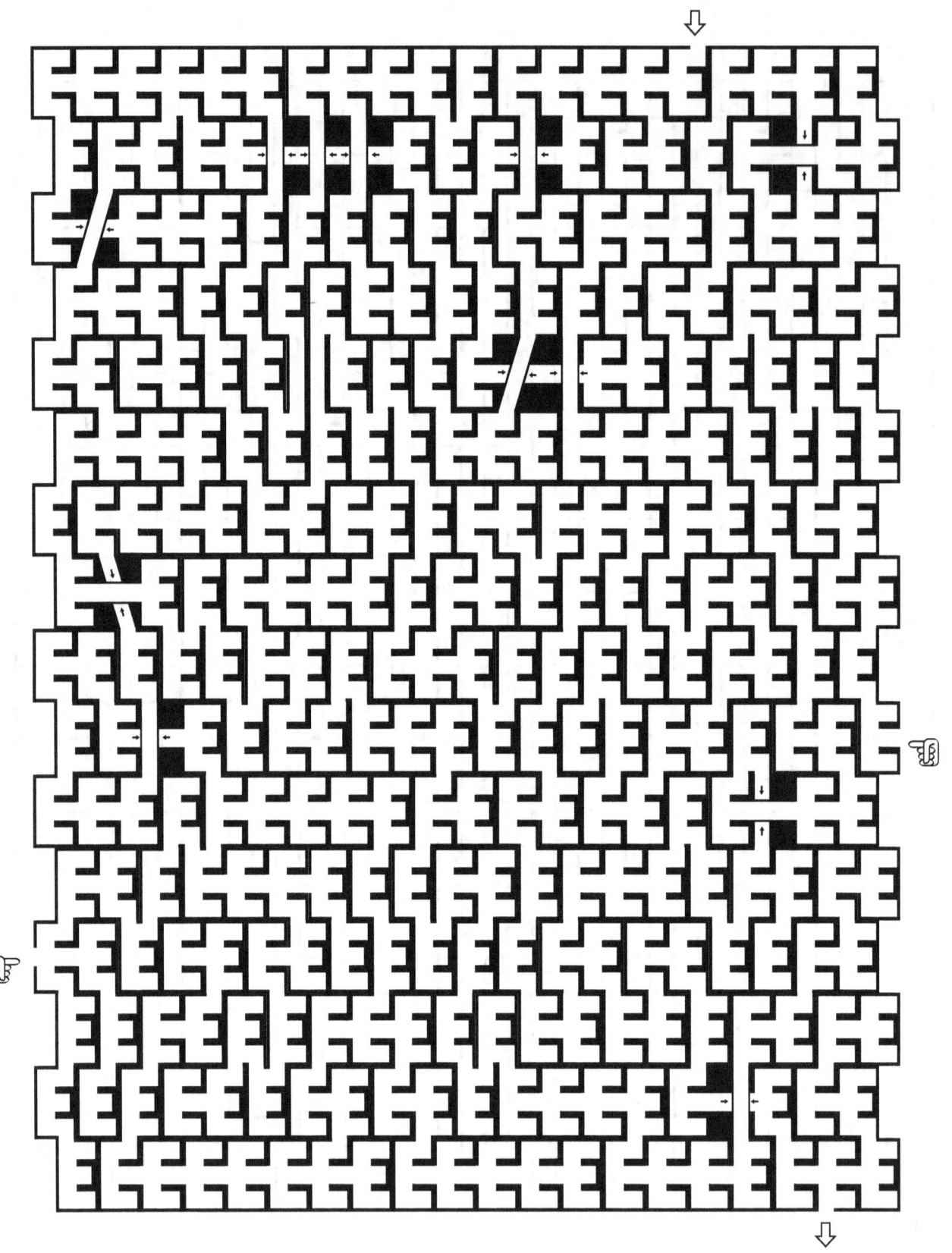

The letter E in another and very different over/under maze.

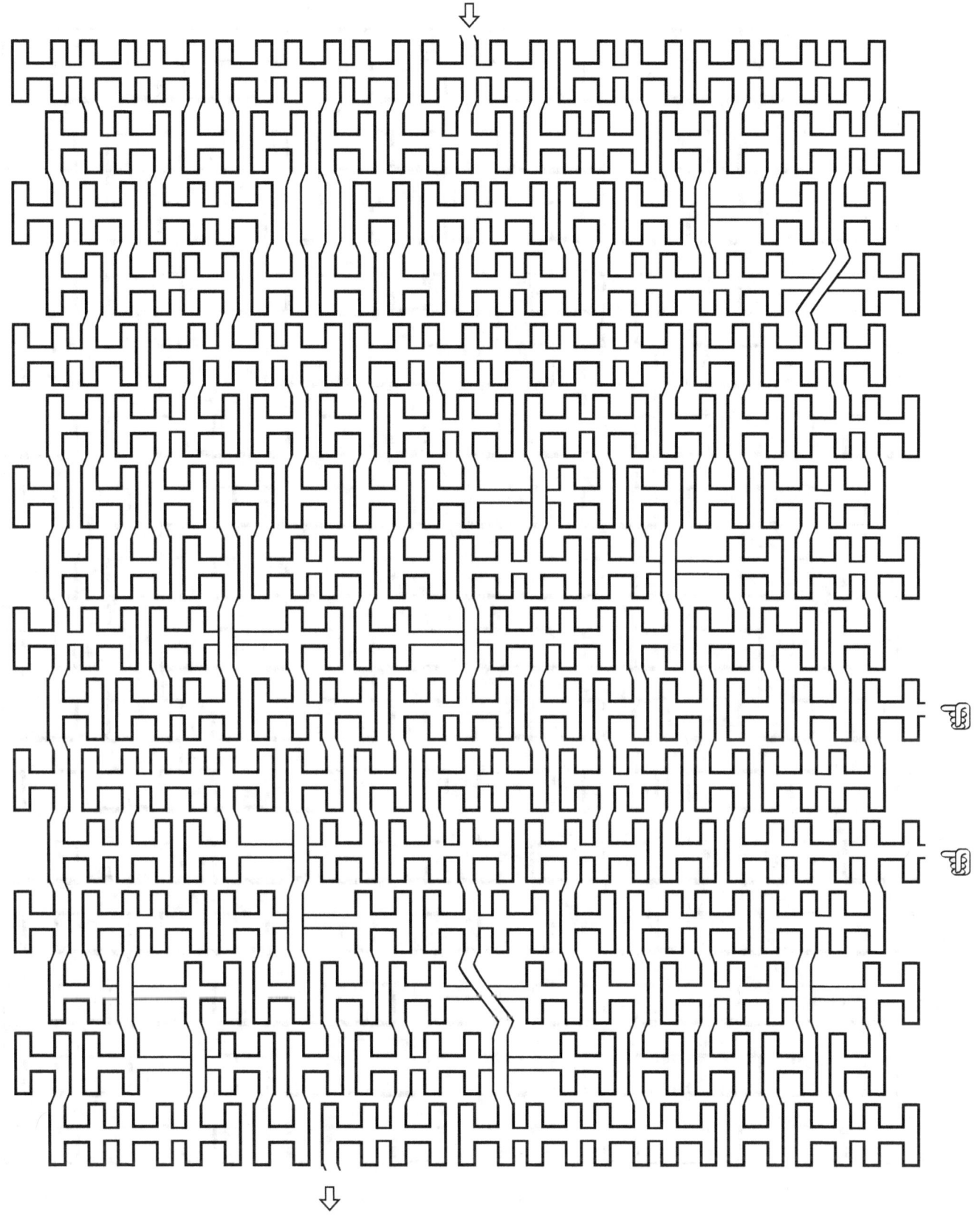

Hexagonal Hs with a twist--it is another over/under maze.

We finish with a couple of tessellations. One little line is all that separates this pattern of tessellating Ts from the pattern of tessellating Is on page 12.

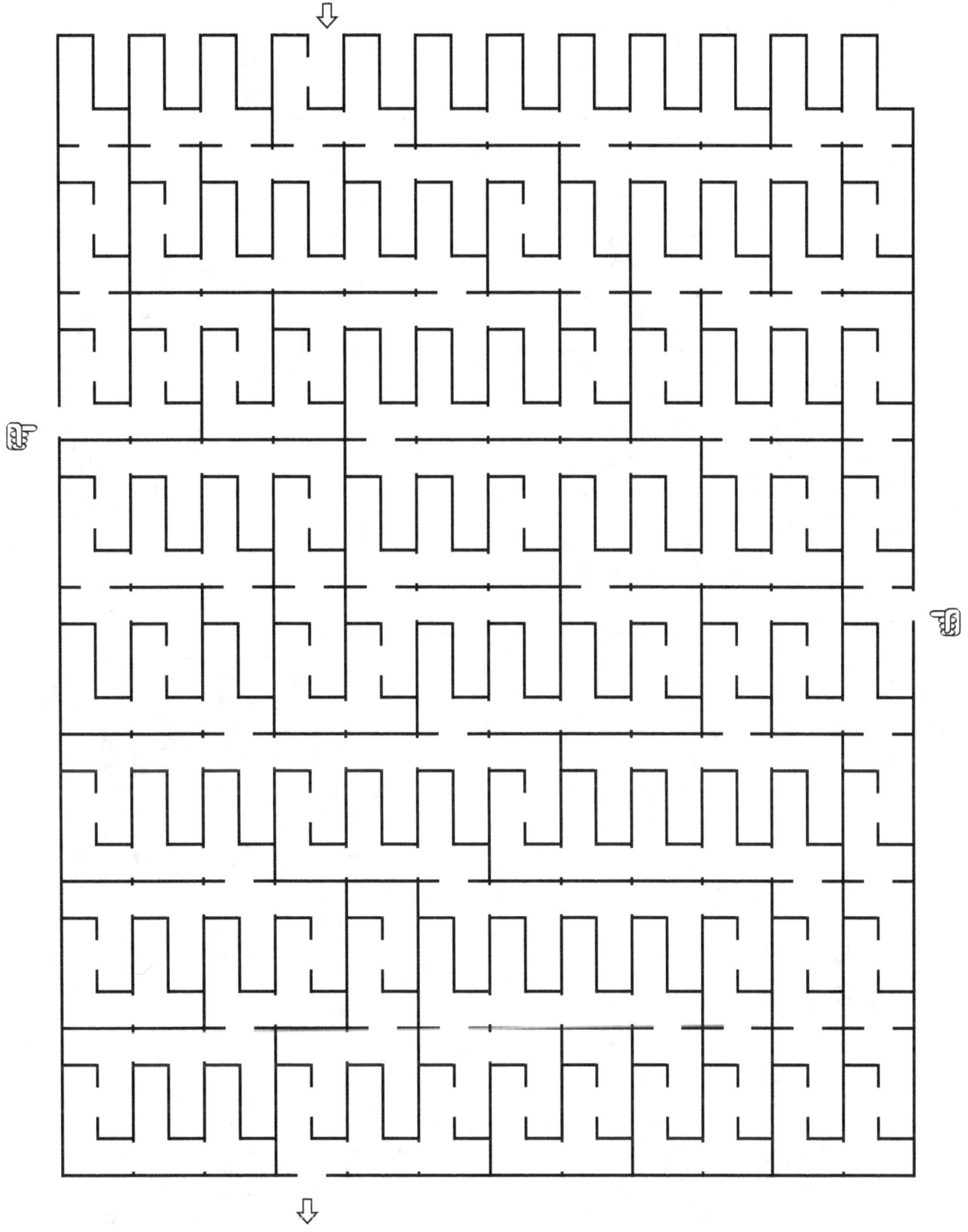

If you are wondering, it is tessellating Ls. The result looks a bit like the maze of tessellating Fs on page 35.

SOLUTIONS

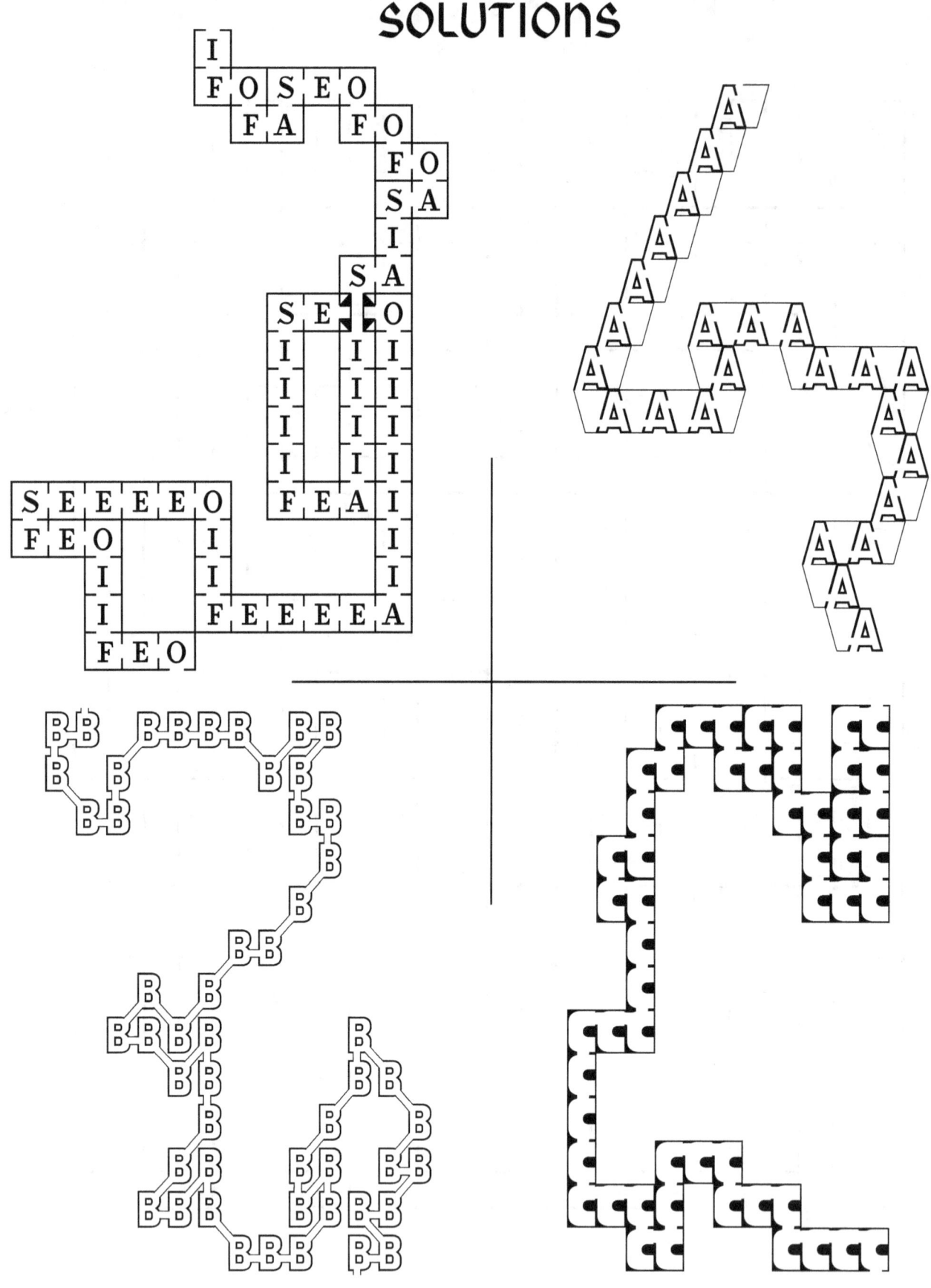

Solutions to mazes on title page, pages 4, 5, and 6.

Solutions to mazes on pages 7, 8, and 9 and 10.

Solutions to mazes on pages 11, 12, 13, and 14.

Solutions to mazes on pages 15, 16, 17, and 18.

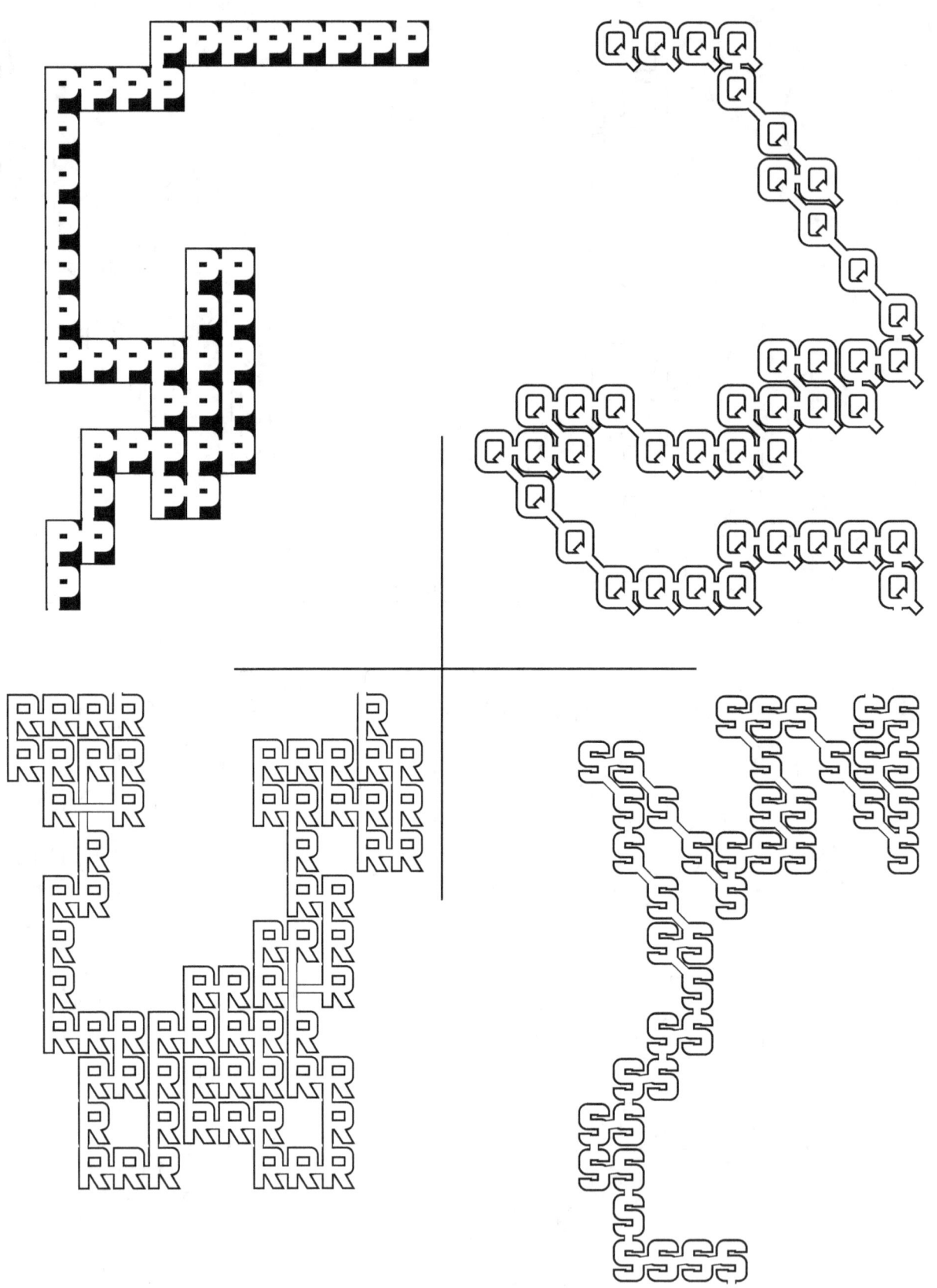

Solutions to mazes on pages 19, 20, 21, and 22

Solutions to mazes on pages 23, 24, 25, and 26.

Solutions to mazes on pages 27, 28, 29, and 30.

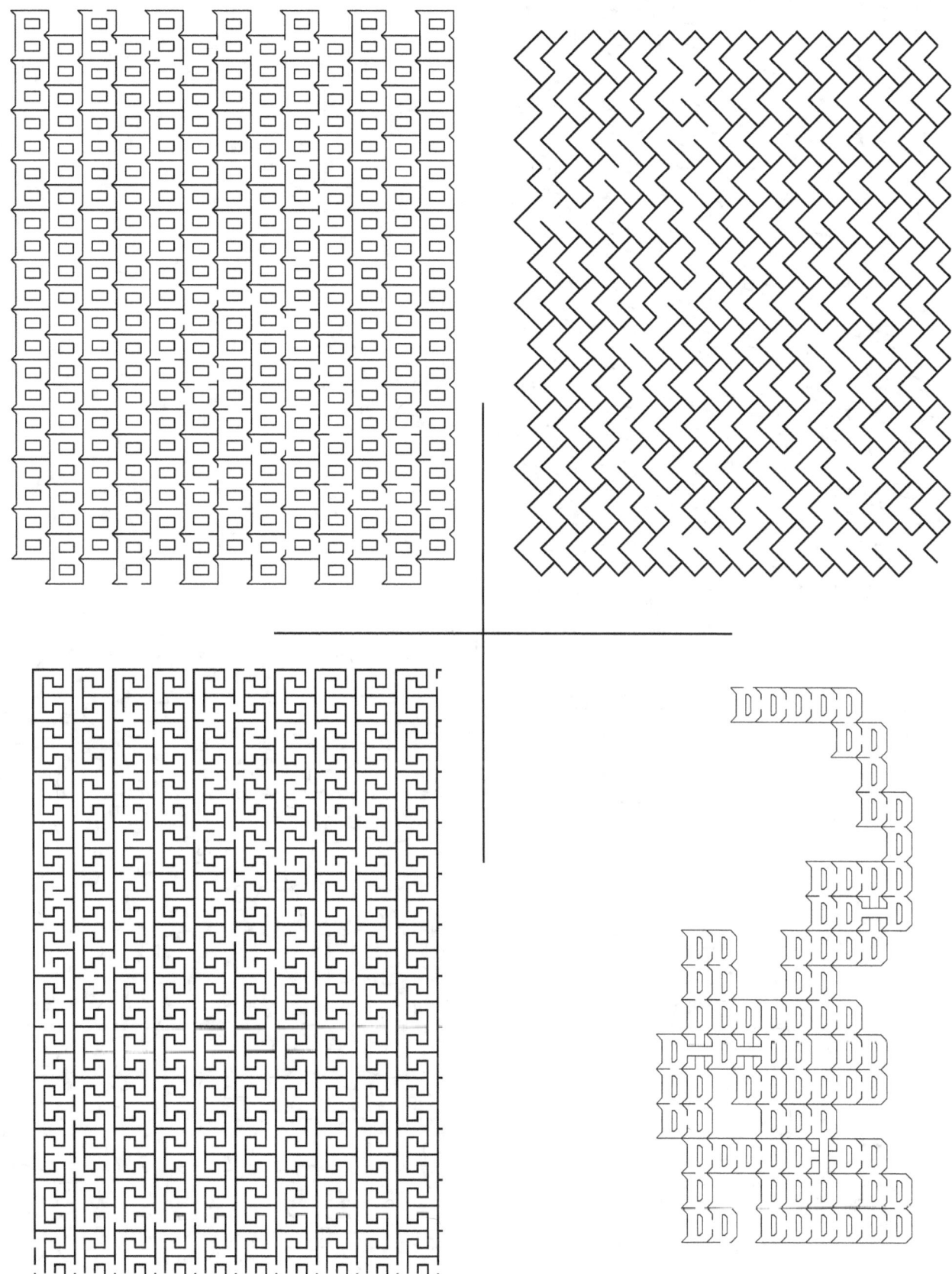

Solutions to mazes on pages 31, 32, 33, and 34.

Solutions to mazes on pages 35, 36, 37, and 38.

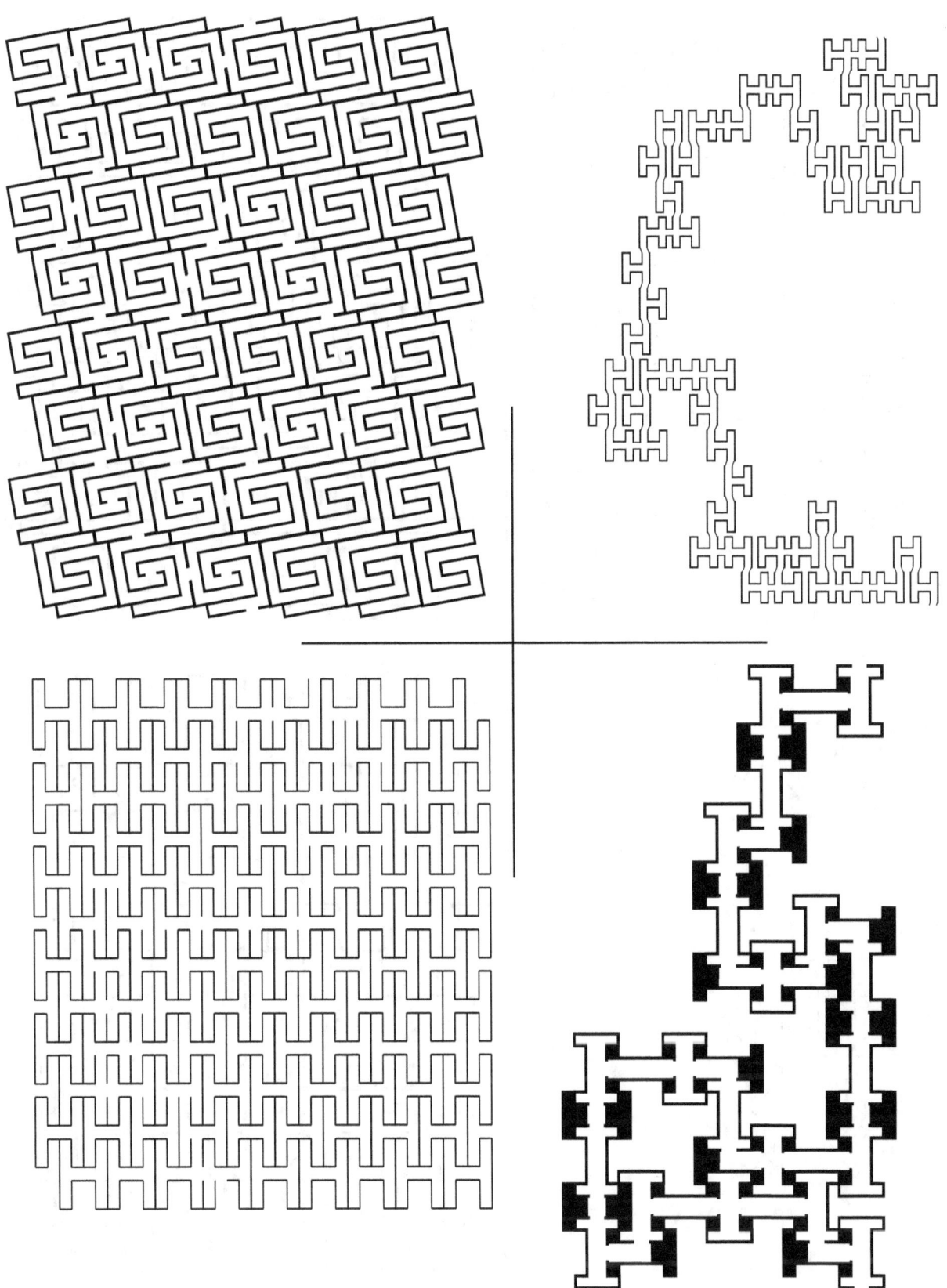

Solutions to mazes on pages 39, 40, 41, and 42.

Solutions to mazes on pages 43, 44, 45, and 46.

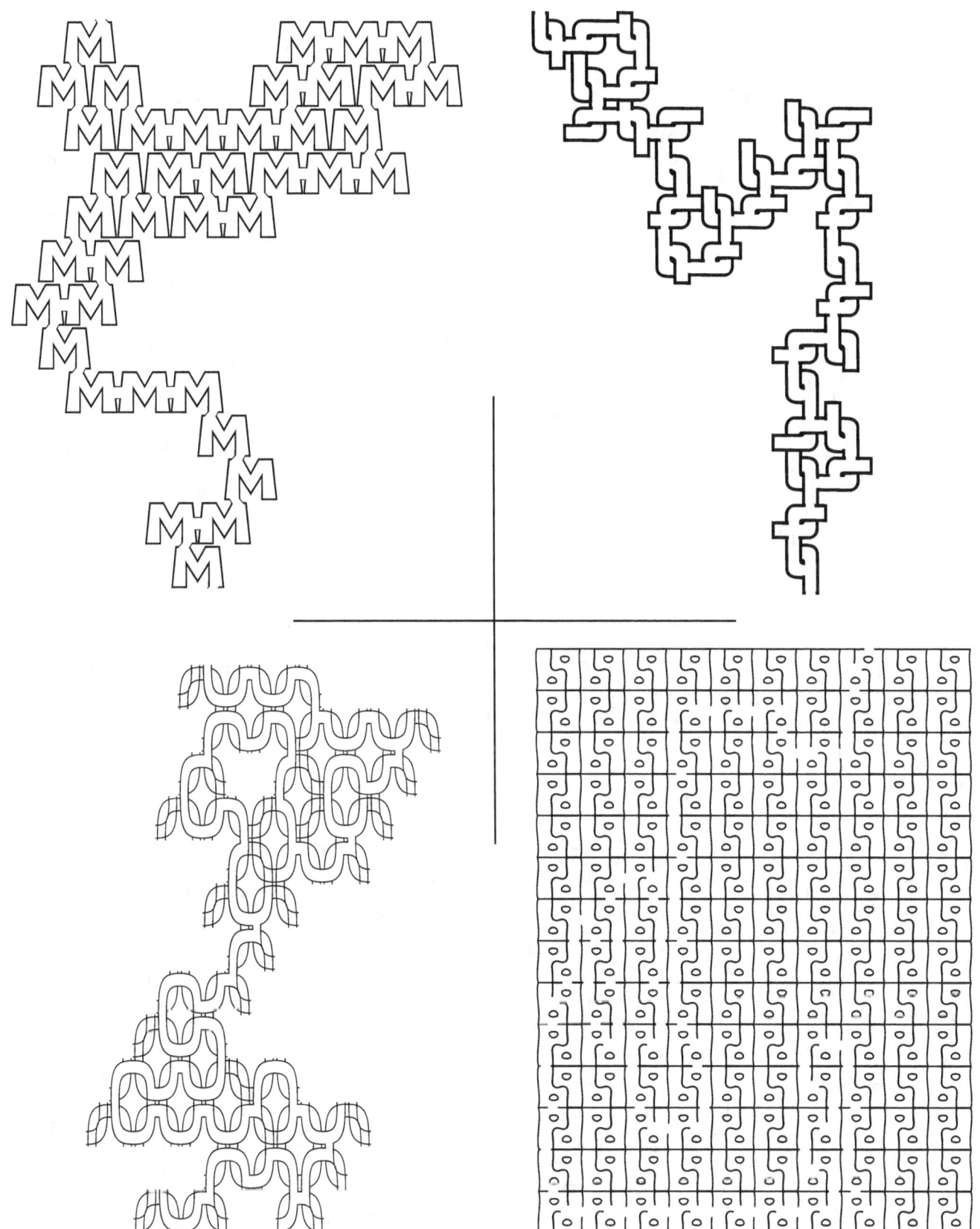

Solutions to mazes on pages 47, 48, 49, and 50.

Solutions to mazes on pages 51, 52, 53, and 54.

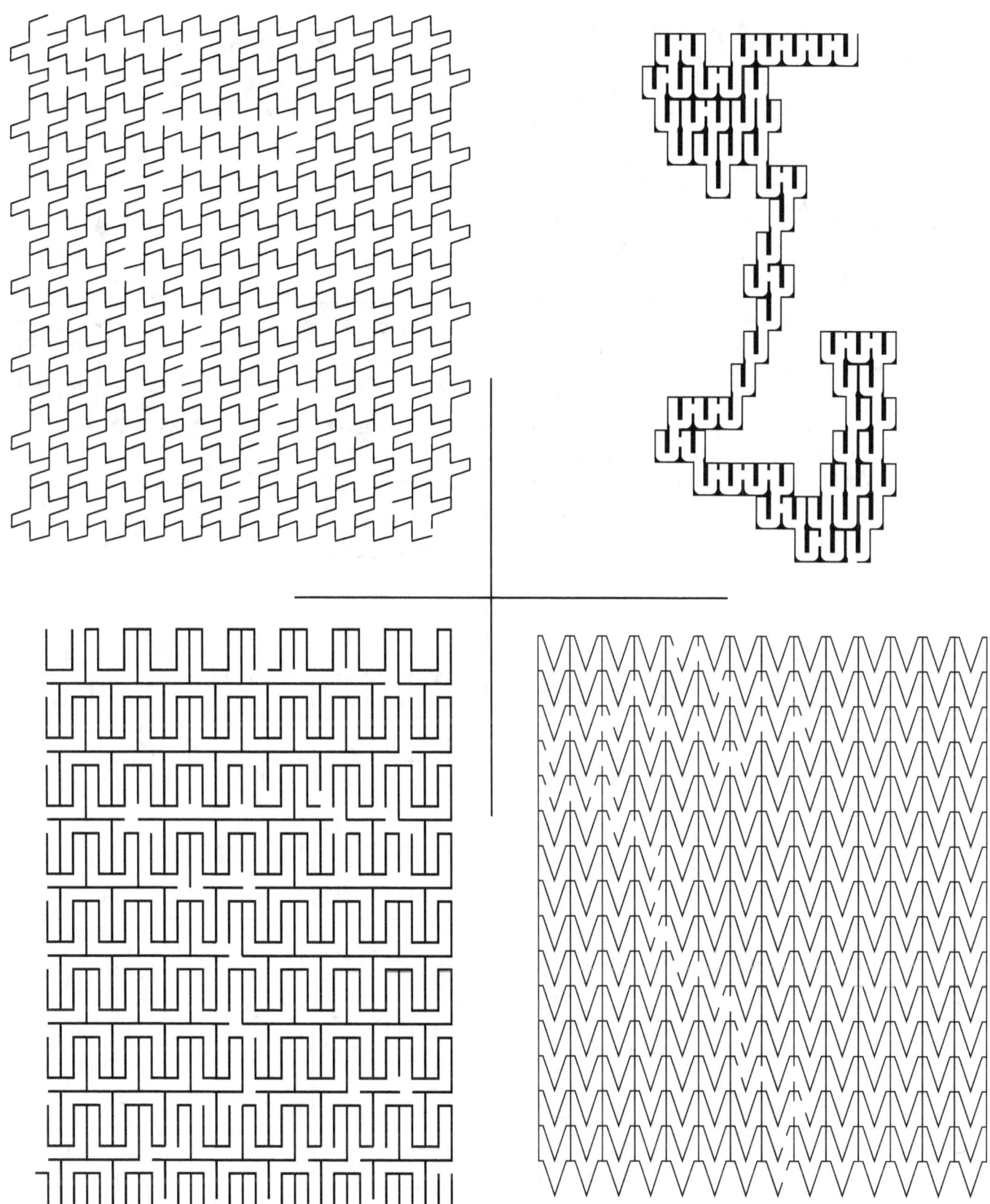

Solutions to mazes on pages 55, 56, 57, and 58.

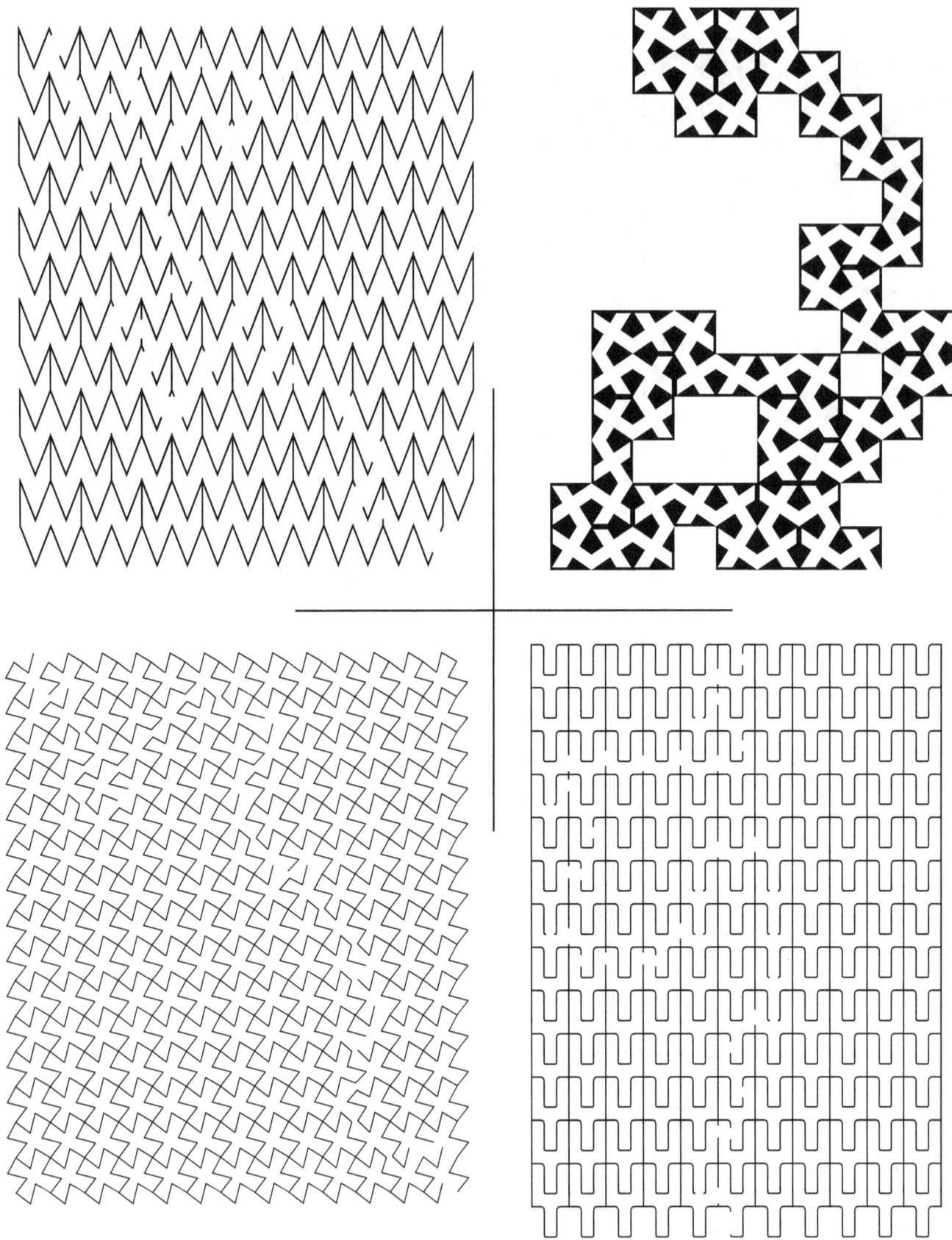

Solutions to mazes on pages 59, 60, 61, and 62.

Solutions to mazes on pages 63, 64, and 65.

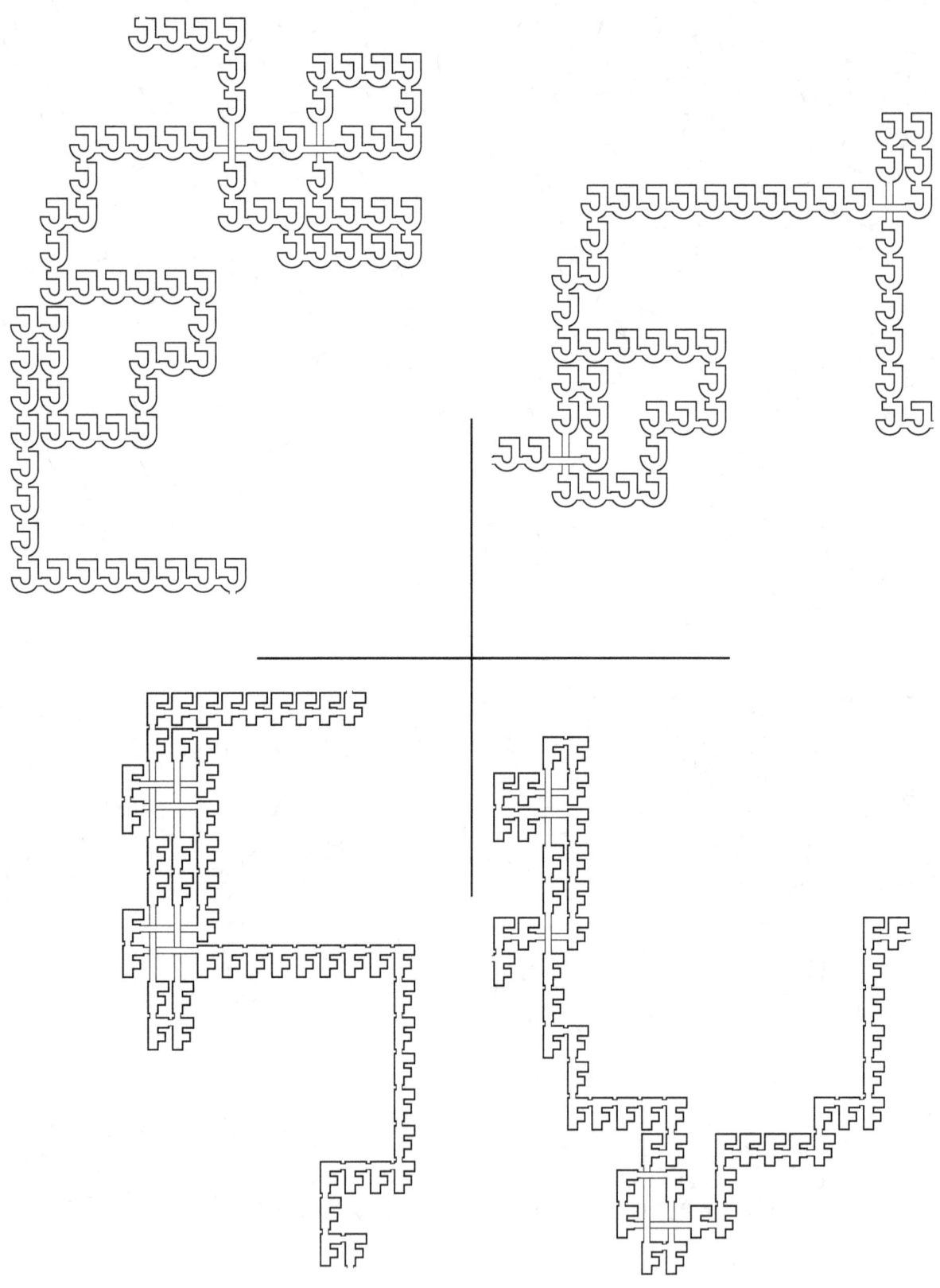

Solutions to mazes on pages 66 and 67.

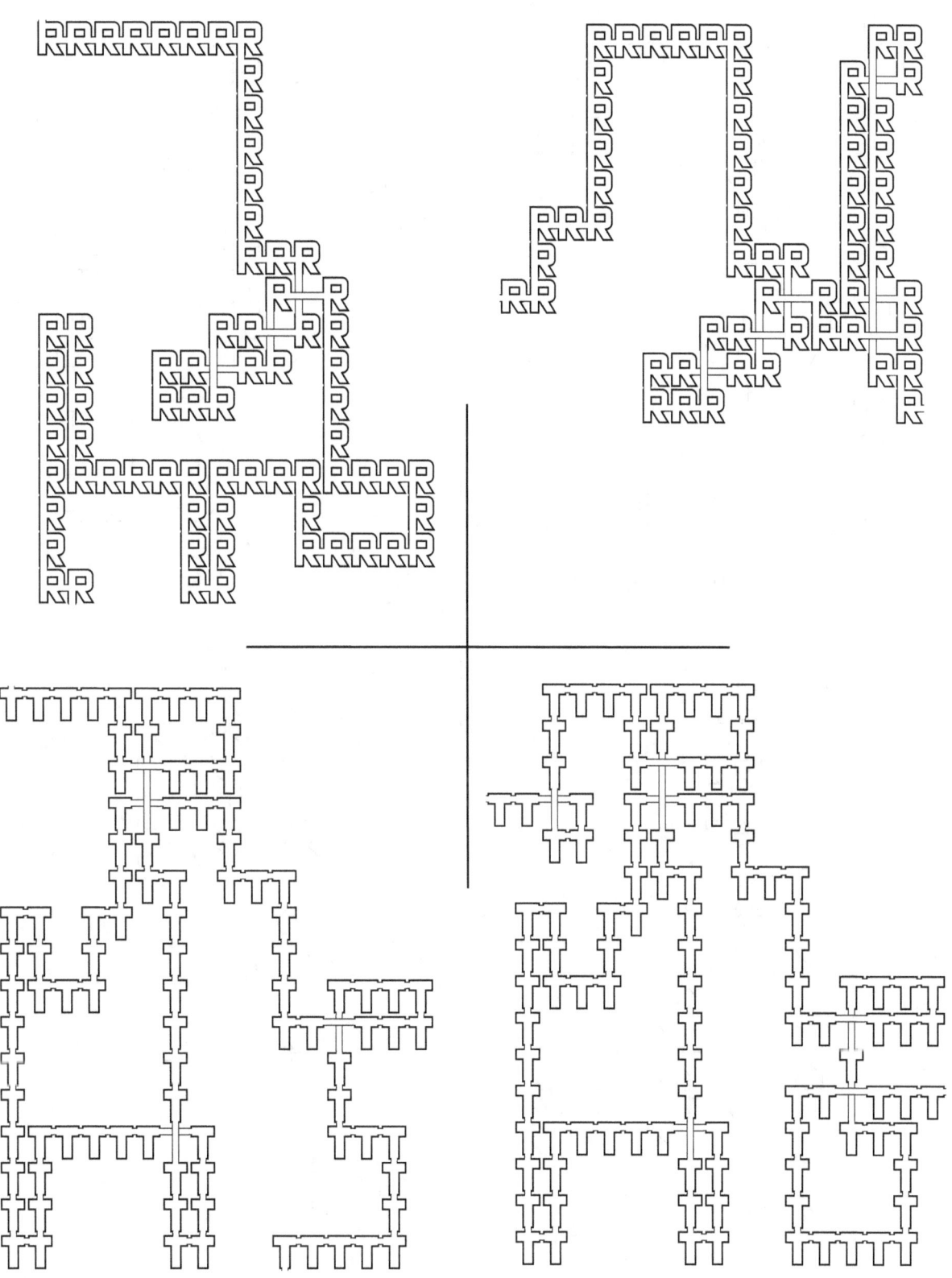

Solutions to mazes on pages 68 and 69.

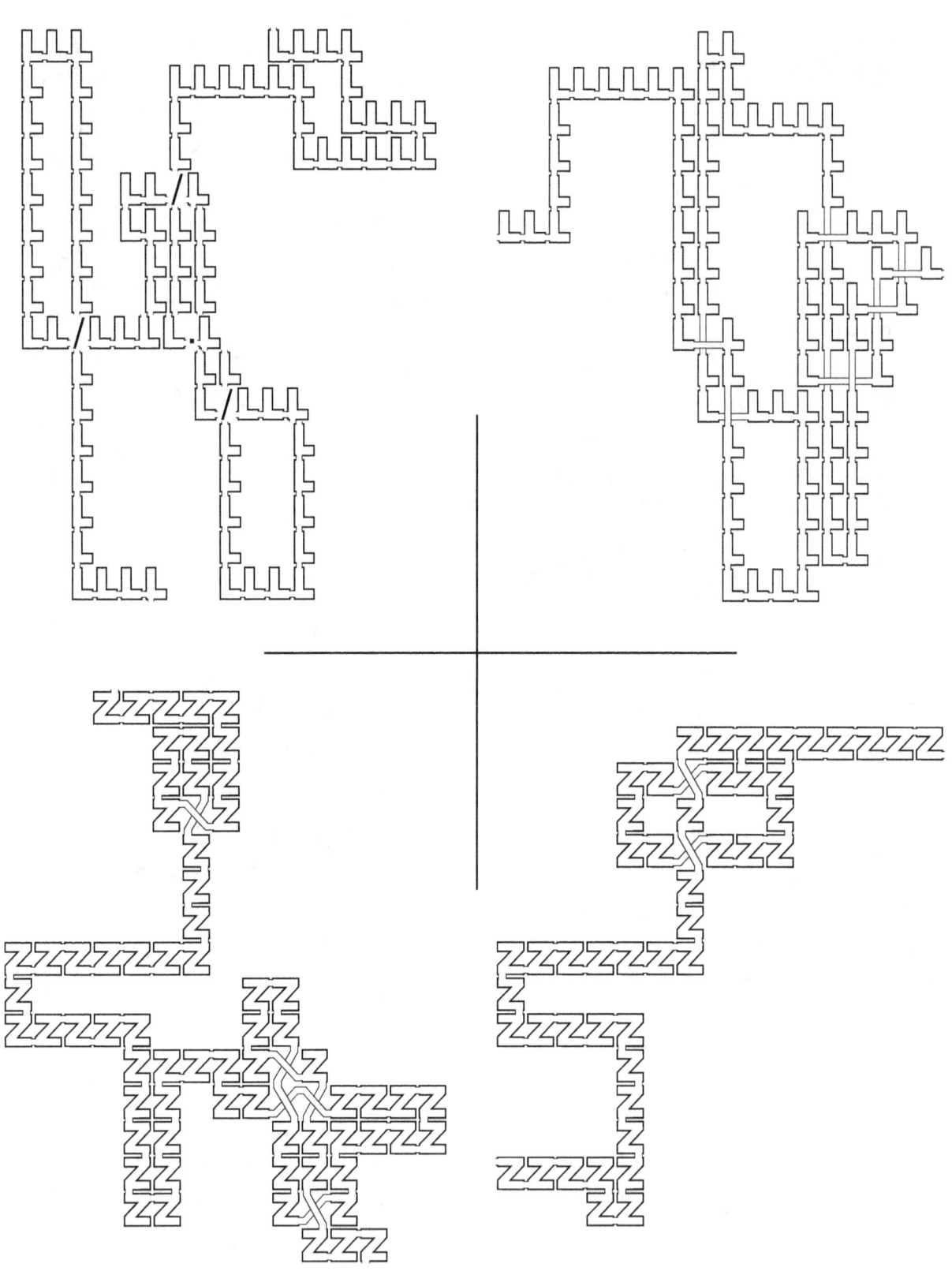

Solutions to mazes on pages 70 and 71.

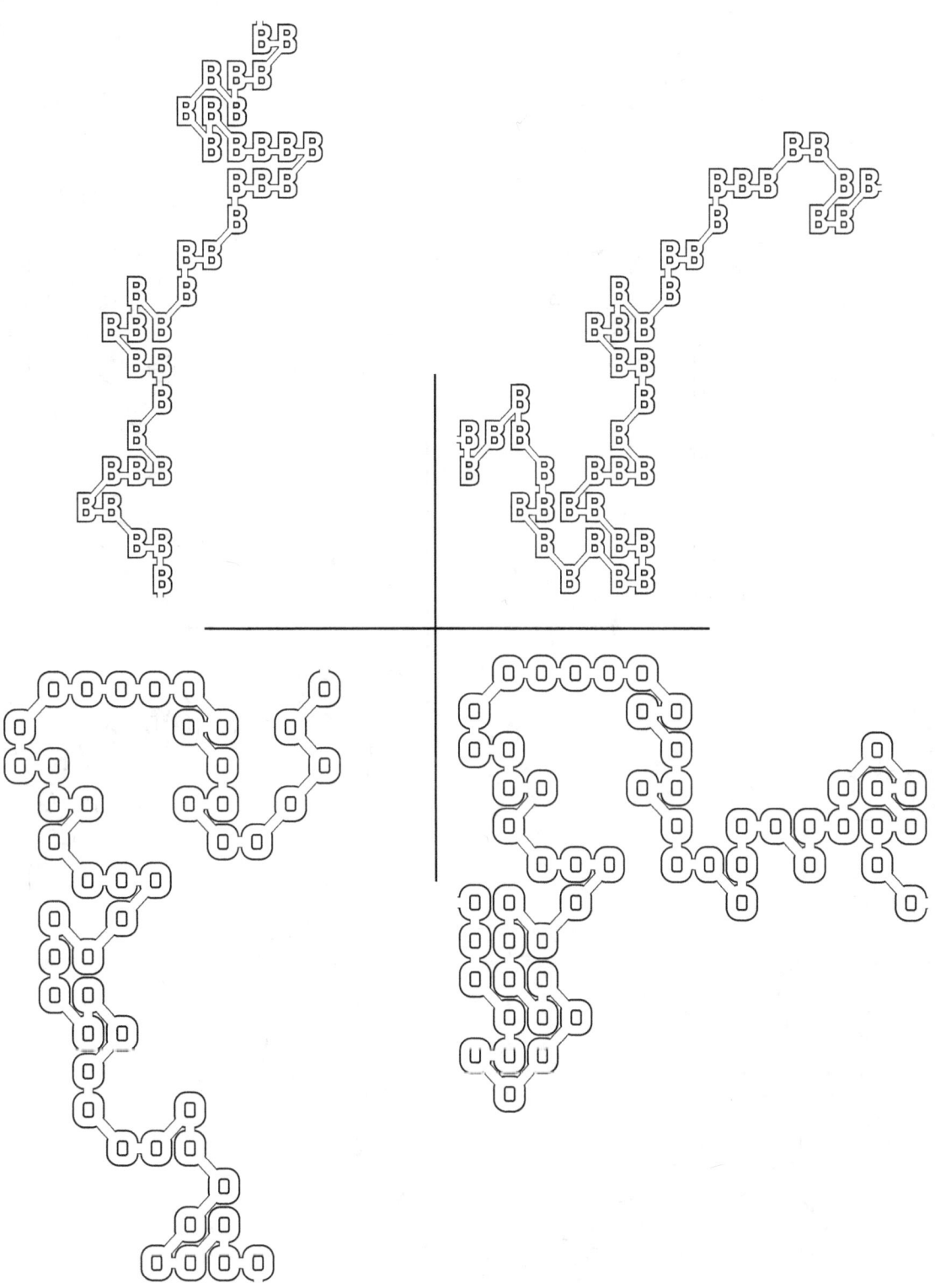

Solutions to mazes on pages 72 and 73.

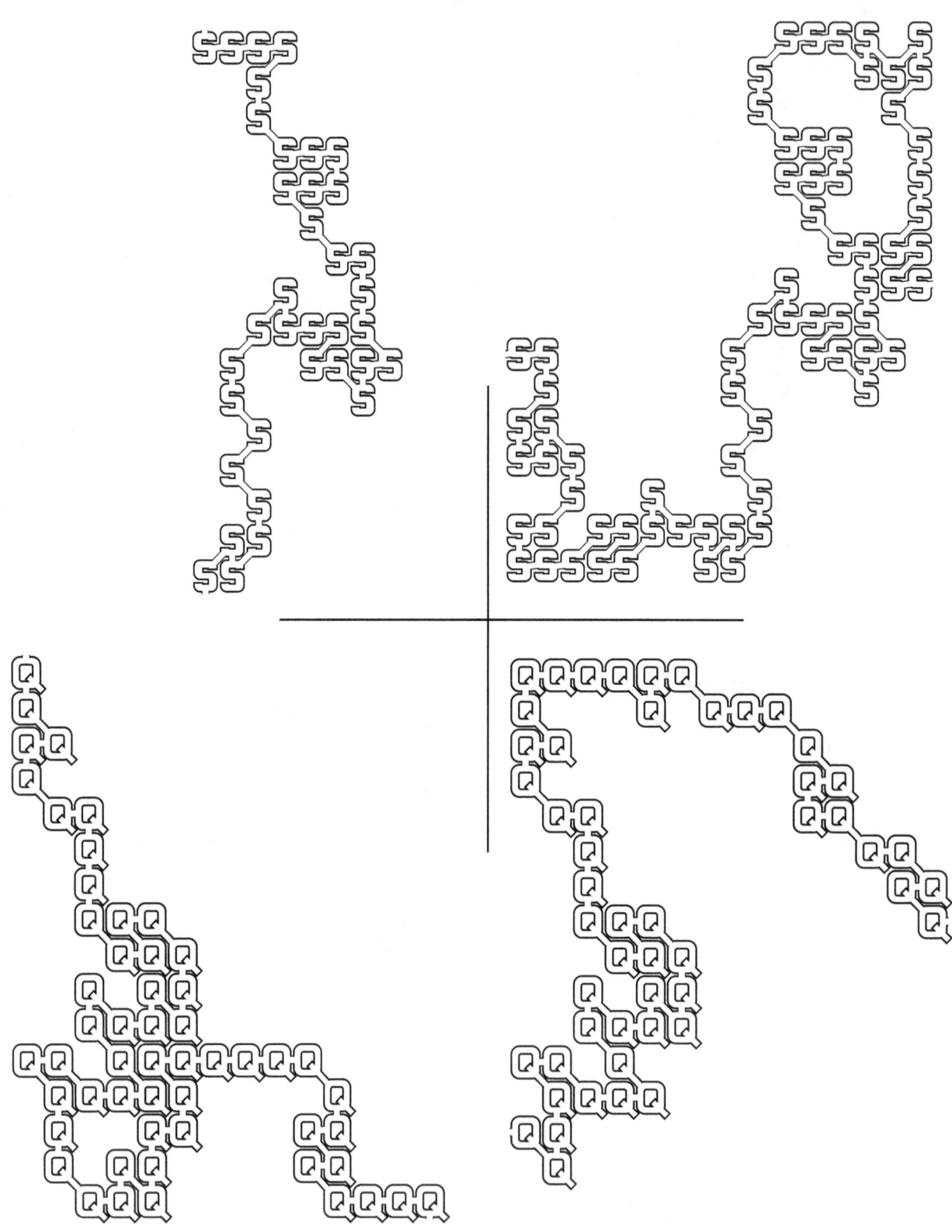

Solutions to mazes on pages 74 and 75.

104

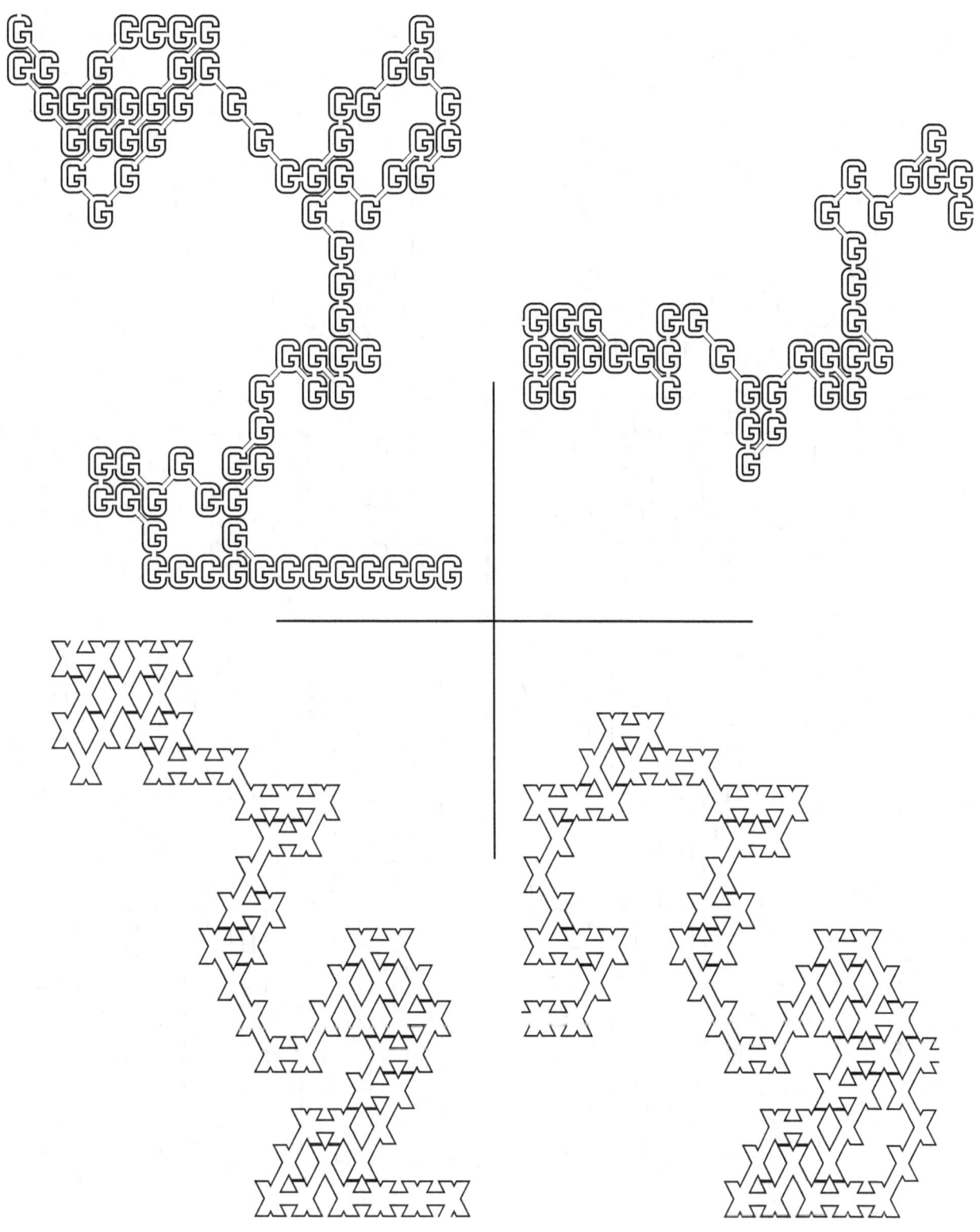

Solutions to mazes on pages 76 and 77.

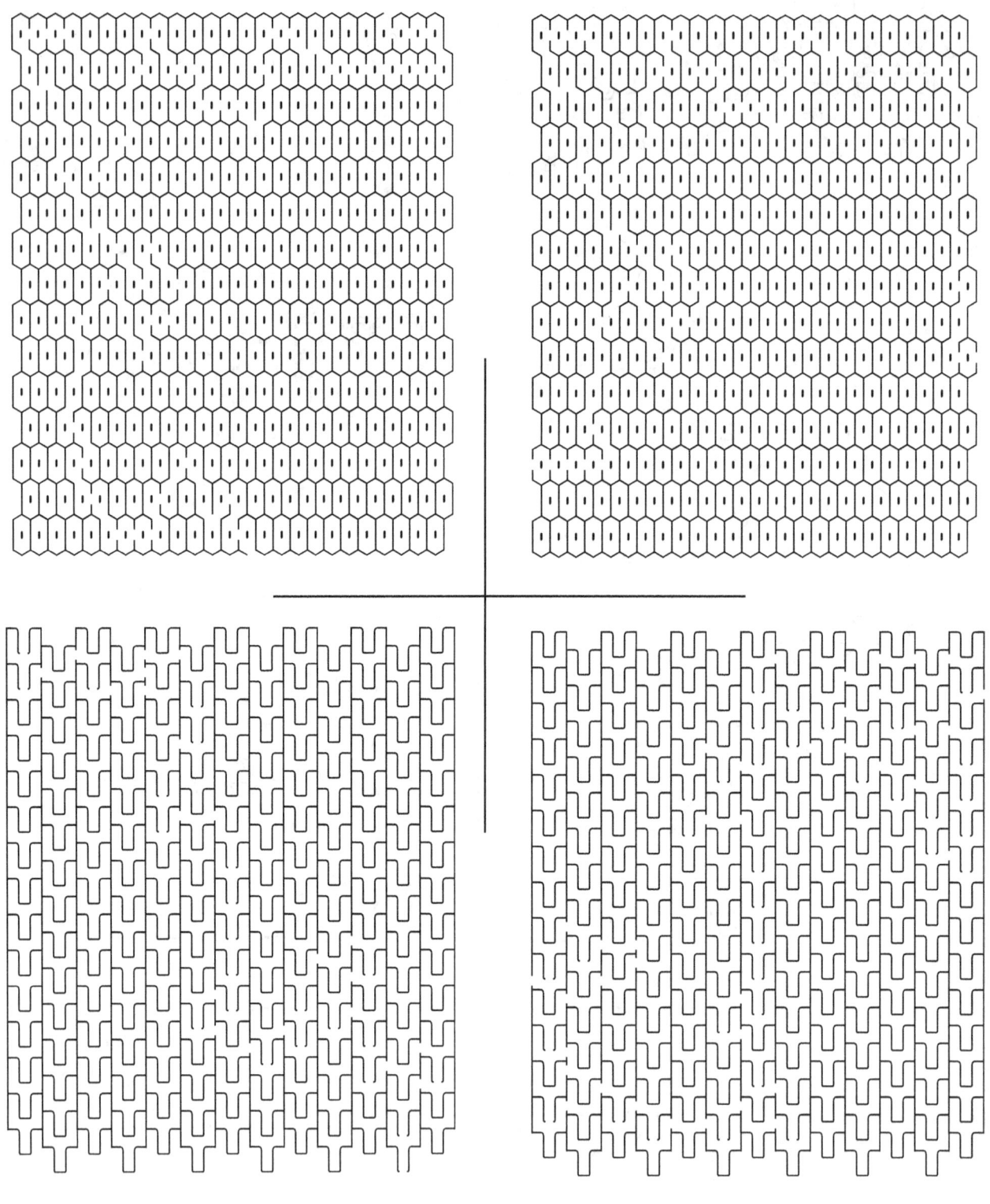

Solutions to mazes on pages 78 and 79.

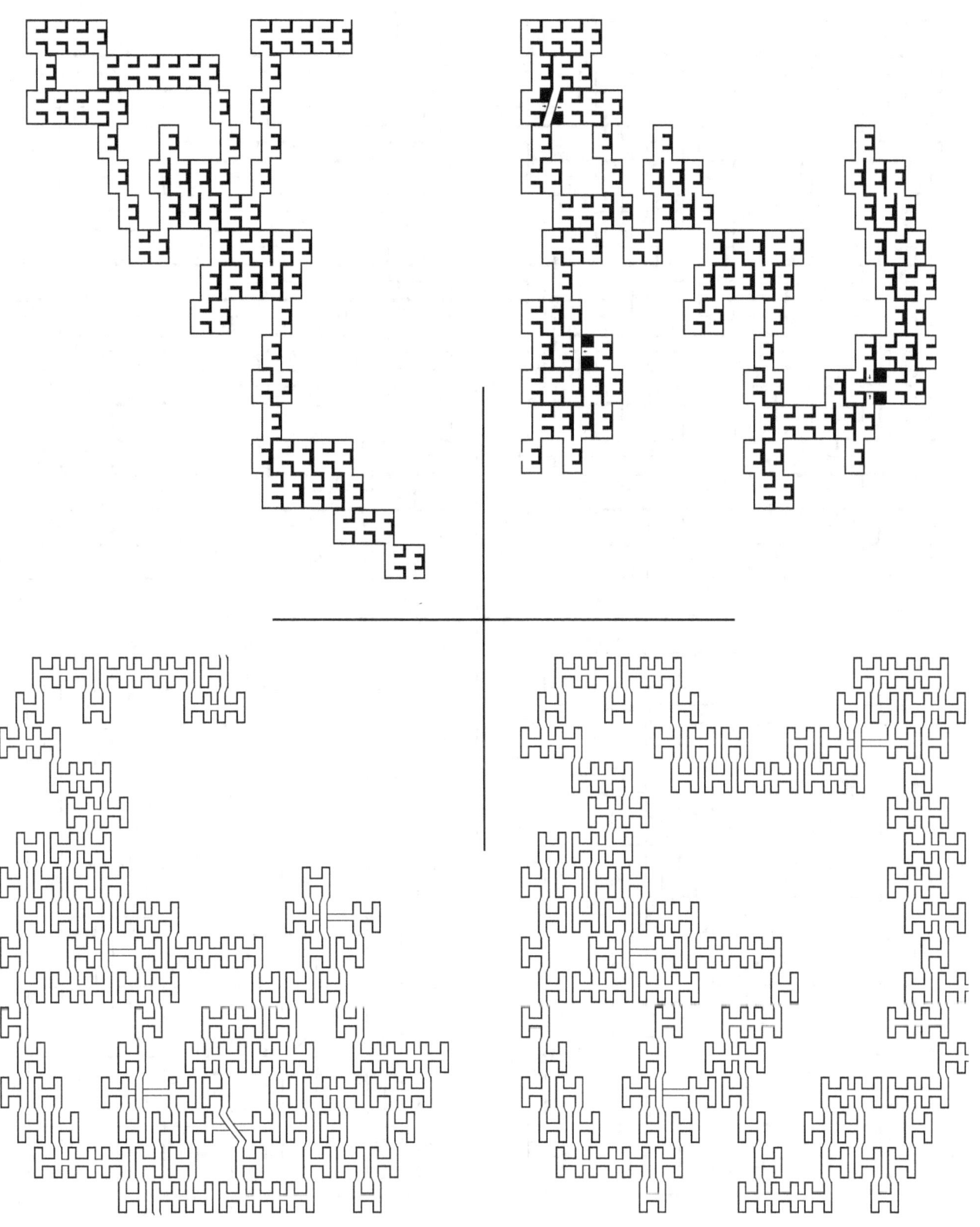

Solutions to mazes on pages 80 and 81.

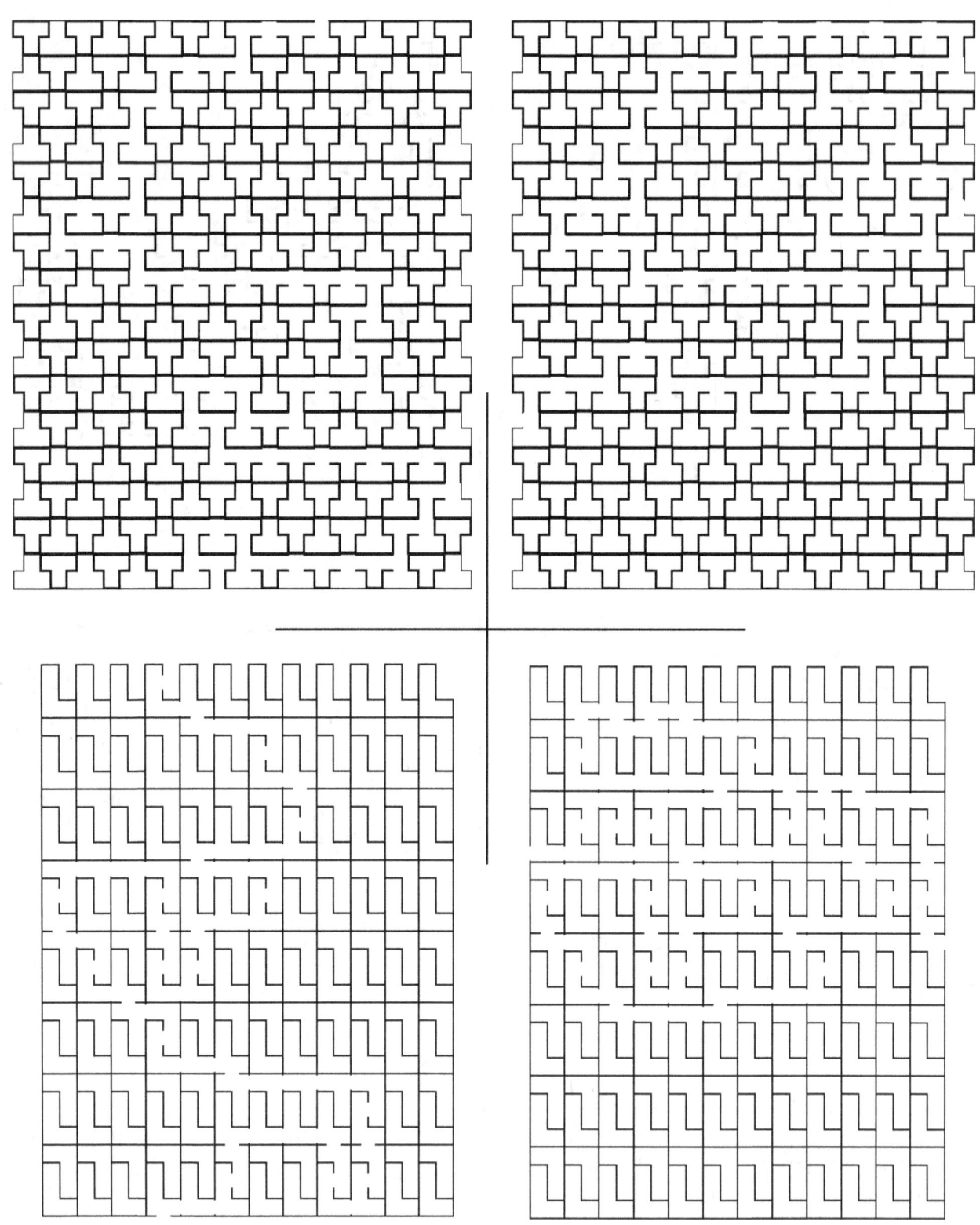

Solutions to mazes on pages 82 and 83.